NANCY ALDEN
COFOUNDER OF BEADWORKS

SIMPLY PEARLS

DESIGNS FOR CREATING PERFECT PEARL JEWELRY

POTTER
CRAFT

NEW YORK

Published in the United States by Potter Craft,
an imprint of the Crown Publishing Group, a division of Random House, Inc., New York.

www.crownpublishing.com
www.clarksonpotter.com

POTTER CRAFT and CLARKSON N. POTTER are trademarks,
and POTTER and colophon are registered trademarks of Random House, Inc.

Library of Congress Cataloging-in-Publication Data is available upon request.

ISBN-10: 0-307-33949-1

Printed in Singapore

Design by Lauren Monchik
Photography by Joseph De Leo

10 9 8 7 6 5 4 3 2 1

First Edition

SIMPLY PEARLS

DESIGNS FOR CREATING PERFECT PEARL JEWELRY

CONTENTS

INTRODUCTION

Who would have thought that a jewel that has been worn since the beginning of history would enter its most vibrant age in the twenty-first century? Yet that is what has happened to pearls, the most ancient of gemstones. Prized for their beauty and their rarity throughout recorded history, they have suddenly acquired a renewed vitality in the imagination of jewelry designers and in the eyes of their admirers. The reason for this is very simple: supply.

Several times in past years, it seemed pearls would become too rare and too expensive for anyone but the wealthy and that demand would inevitably outstrip the dwindling supply of natural pearls. Each time, human ingenuity circumvented the problem. The Chinese first conceived the idea of artificially inducing shellfish to produce pearl shapes, and now China is making pearl beads that are affordable for all.

Just as Japanese cultured saltwater pearls expanded the market at the beginning of the twentieth century, so the Chinese cultured freshwater pearl is expanding it at the beginning of the twenty-first. Only a few years ago, China was belittled for its production of poor quality "seed" pearls. Now, Chinese growers are transforming the industry with their increasingly sophisticated products. In the process, they have reshaped thousands of acres of countryside into watery "fields," each planted with shellfish, and all hard at work creating new pearls. Every year, the "farmers" who tend this crop have discovered new ways to improve its quality, quantity, and variety. We might have predicted that ingenuity would once again provide a way to increase the supply of a desirable product, but the scale of production has been unprecedented and unexpected.

To the surprise and delight of jewelry designers, pearls are now entering the true "golden age" of their immensely long history.

Take advantage of this exciting new supply and variety of pearls. You don't have to be intimidated by price or restricted by a lack of sources anymore. This book will show you how to create your own wonderful pearl jewelry using the tools and techniques favored by professional designers. As you'll see, the projects are neither complicated nor time consuming. After all, a pearl is simply a bead that needs a little special attention!

AN ABUNDANCE OF PEARLS
Contemporary jewelry makers can now find pearls in an astonishing variety of shapes, colors, lusters, and, most importantly, costs. Breathtaking pearls still fetch breathtaking prices, but now entire strands of perfectly pleasing freshwater pearls are available for less than the cost of dinner for two.

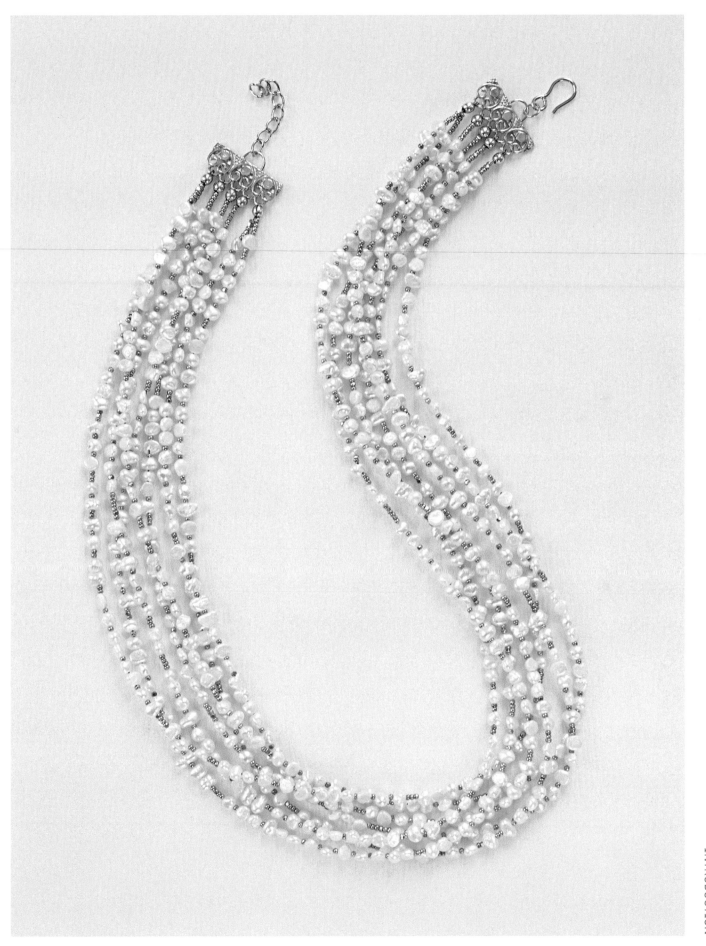

BASICS

WHAT IS A PEARL?

It's ironic to think that a pearl begins life as something irritating! Irritating, that is, to some of the soft-bodied creatures called mollusks. It is even more unlikely that this exquisite gem is the work of a group of animals not famed for their glamour. The mollusks, after all, include slugs and snails as well as the rather more attractive shellfish. It's commonly believed that oysters produce pearls, but this is not, in fact, true. The commonly called "pearl oyster" is not of the Ostreidae family, and it usually only provides us with food for the eye. But let's not quibble over a name—"pearl oyster" sounds much more romantic than "pearl mollusk."

A KNACK FOR NACRE

Wherever they come from, whether they are natural or cultured, saltwater or freshwater, pearls have a common structure and share the same process of creation.

First, an irritant is introduced by accident or design into the mollusk. Presumably in an attempt to live more comfortably with the intruder, the animal then starts coating it with a hard, smooth substance called nacre (pronounced NAY-kur). More and more layers of nacre are deposited and, very slowly, a pearl starts to grow. In this way, the irritant becomes, we assume, more comfortable for the mollusk to live with and also transforms into something we treasure.

While many mollusks can perform this trick, what distinguishes valuable pearls from bits of dull, unwanted stone is the quality of the nacre covering. Some species just have a special knack for making a coat of iridescent magic. They don't do this exclusively to deal with annoying specks of grit, either. The entire inner lining of their shell is covered with this wonderful substance, giving us mother-of-pearl— another marvelous element for the jeweler's art.

THE SCIENCE BEHIND THE BEAUTY

Nacre itself is composed of two main substances: aragonite and conchiolin. Aragonite is a crystalline form of calcium carbonate, a very common mineral that makes up limestone, coral reefs, and shells. In a small way, shell-making mollusks are doing their bit for the environment since every molecule of calcium carbonate they make removes one of carbon dioxide from the atmosphere. Conchiolin, a more complex substance, is a glue-like protein that is excreted by the

SHAPE

The great majority of natural pearls are anything but round. That is why a strand of round, natural pearls of the same size and shape is so phenomenally expensive— it could take years to collect a set. Fortunately, all the different shapes of pearls can be just as attractive as rounds; sometimes, they are even more interesting.

THE OYSTER MYTH

Pearls are produced by a number of saltwater and freshwater shellfish. The famous sea-dwelling pearl makers are mostly of the genus Pinctada, although several other salt-water shellfish such as abalone and conch also create pearls. (Some would say that conchs do not make real pearls as they are not nacreous.) Indeed, the largest pearl in the world, a fourteen-pound, football-sized monster, was found in a giant clam. What comes as a surprise to many, however, is that a great number of pearls have always come from shellfish that live in rivers and lakes. No one even claims that these are oysters; we refer to them instead as pearl mussels. As modern pearl production focuses more and more on freshwater sources, the chances are ever greater that your pearls will have been produced by a humble mussel.

mollusk and binds together the aragonite crystals like bricks in a wall. Of course, this layering and coating process does not necessarily produce pearls that are round. But the unique way in which these translucent aragonite crystals are deposited gives the coating its ability to reflect and refract light. And it is this play of light that makes the pearl a gem. Because the nacre is translucent, light can reflect off the exterior surface as well as from layers just beneath the surface. This gives the pearl its particular warmth and depth—a unique luster unlike that of any other gemstone.

The different colors of pearls, which range from almost white to almost black, are often naturally occurring. Like most gemstones, however, the natural colors are sometimes enhanced through bleaching, heating, or even dyeing. If this is done within reasonable and customary limits, it is considered an agreeable way to treat a pearl. However, aggressive methods that could do long-term damage to the nacre, along with methods that make the enhancement impermanent, are only acceptable in the cheapest pearls.

Whatever the variety—round or baroque, white or peacock blue, breathtakingly expensive or astonishingly cheap—the pearl is an ideal material for the jewelry designer's art. When displayed in the right setting, it has few rivals for attention.

THE VARIETIES OF PEARLS

NATURAL PEARLS
Today it is rare to find pearls for sale that have not been cultured. If you are lucky enough to have inherited a strand of natural pearls or acquired some in an estate sale, treat them with respect, but don't tuck them away in some hidden drawer. Pearls benefit from being worn. When you are confident enough in your design abilities, you might want to restring an old necklace to make a new, modern piece.

AKOYA PEARLS
Akoyas are round pearls cultured in the saltwater mollusk *Pinctada fucata*. Traditionally regarded as an exclusively Japanese product, large quantities of Akoya pearls are now produced in China. The nucleus of these pearls is a round bead made from the shell of an American mussel. As with all nucleated pearls, the layers of nacre can vary according to the length of time the pearl is left to grow. Generally, the higher the number of nacre layers, the better the quality. Akoyas are seldom more than 9 millimeters in size.

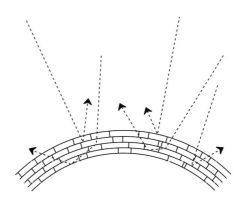
How pearls reflect light.

NACRE COATING
The thickness of the nacre coating is extremely important to a pearl's value. Thick layers give the pearl more luster and greater longevity. Since freshwater, non-nucleated pearls are all nacre, the question of coating thickness does not arise. In nucleated pearls, however, producers have to compromise between the number of layers a mollusk will coat around the nucleus and the length of time they must leave it in the water to do its work.

PEARL STRAND KEY (PAGES 12–13, FROM LEFT TO RIGHT)
1. Tahitian Black Baroque
2. Akoya Near Round
3. Silver-Rice
4. Pink Potato
5. Drops
6. Seed
7. Top-Drilled Button
8. Top-Drilled Drop
9. Side-Drilled Potato
10. Lilac Near Round
11. Akoya Round
12. Facetted Round
13. Mixed Peach, Pink, Lilac, White Top-Drilled Peanut
14. Keshi
15. Stick
16. Coin

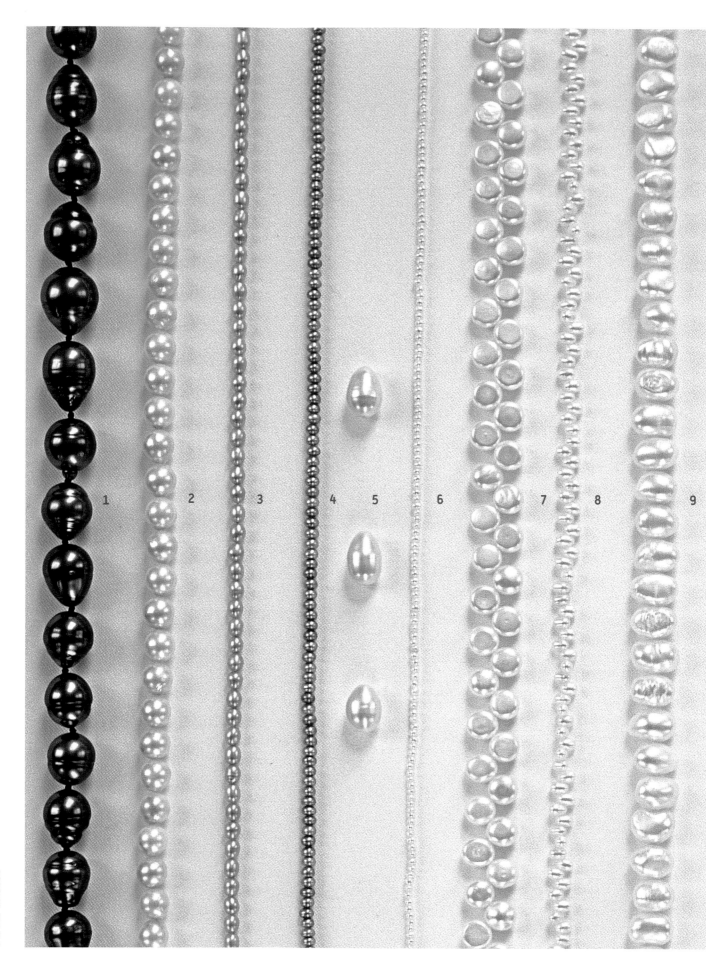

1   2   3   4   5   6   7   8   9

10   11   12   13   14   15   16

SOUTH SEA PEARLS

These pearls are cultured in the South Pacific, particularly in Australia but also in Indonesia and the Philippines. They are nucleated in the same way as Akoyas and come in round or baroque (round but irregular) shapes. Grown in the *Pinctada maxima* mollusk, South Sea pearls are the largest of any commercially traded pearls, commonly measuring between 10 millimeters and 15 millimeters in size. It is not unheard of for South Sea pearls to reach more than 20 millimeters, but their cost increases dramatically in extremely large sizes.

TAHITIAN PEARLS

These large pearls are from the *Pinctada margaritifera*, or black-lipped oyster, the creature that produces the famous "black" pearls of the South Sea Islands. In reality, the colors of Tahitian pearls are not black but a subtle range of iridescent shades from a metallic gray to eggplant purple. Not all black pearls are Tahitian, however; instead, many are dyed pearls from other sources.

KESHI PEARLS

Keshis are serendipitous accidents of the culturing process. Occasionally, parts of the originally implanted mantle tissue break away and start forming separate irregular pearls of their own. There are also times when the nucleus bead is rejected altogether, leaving just the mantle implant to grow a freestyle pearl. Since the shapes have a wonderful variety and their all-nacre composition often gives them great luster and orient, keshi pearls have become much appreciated by jewelry designers.

FRESHWATER PEARLS

The culturing of freshwater pearls began in Lake Biwa in Japan in the 1930s. These "all-nacre" gems became so popular that the name "Biwa" has often been mistakenly used to denote any freshwater pearl. Due to pollution of the water, Lake Biwa produces very few pearls today. Luckily, the growing sophistication and quantity of Chinese freshwater pearls has brought prices back to levels that are attractive to a wide international market and has also led to a rapid increase in availability and variety.

While two decades ago the Chinese were producing tiny irregular pearls, scornfully dubbed "Rice Krispies" by the major players in the pearl market, they are now creating round, all-nacre pearls that rival Japanese Akoyas. Barring environmental disaster, it's likely that more and more of the pearls we wear will be coming from China.

FARM FRESH

Large-scale production of freshwater pearls has almost wholly shifted to the scattered patchwork of ponds that makes up China's pearl-farm industry.

JEWELRY-MAKING SUPPLIES

Before you rush out to buy any of the items listed below, carefully read the list of necessary ingredients and tools for the project you have in mind. Some require very few tools or materials. In recent years, the proliferation of bead stores around the world has made it easy to acquire jewelry-making supplies. If you do not have a local bead store, there are large numbers of mail-order suppliers, most of whom offer online shopping via their websites.

TOOLS

It's surprising how few tools you need to make jewelry. For the simple stringing of pearls, you can get away with just two: a beading needle and an awl. The other tools you will need to make the designs in this book are detailed in "Toolbox Essentials" listed below.

Some of these items you can find around the house, but you'll want to make a modest investment in tools specifically designed for jewelry makers, since they will make your life easier and your finished jewelry better.

There are other specialty items you can add as you go along, but the items in "Toolbox Essentials" are all you really need. Some people like to lay out their necklaces on a bead design board that has specially designed curved channels for holding beads. If you don't want to purchase one, you'll need to work with a bead mat or some other thick, soft material to keep your beads from rolling all over the place.

Like everything in life, beading tools come in levels of quality. Their cost depends on precision, sturdiness, and durability. If you are on a budget or think that your enthusiasm for making jewelry might be short-lived, you can buy cheap pliers to get yourself started. When you are hooked by the satisfaction and pleasure of creating your own jewelry, it will be time to upgrade—look for tools made in Germany. Once a passion for the craft sets in, you might want to splash out on a really superb set of Swedish cutters and pliers. But the important thing is just to get started.

SPACERS

Spacers are just beads that create spaces between other larger or more important beads. Theoretically, all beads can act as spacers.

TOOLBOX ESSENTIALS

- Wire cutters
- Narrow flat-nosed pliers (also known as chain-nosed pliers)
- Round-nosed pliers
- An awl
- Crimping pliers (only for designs that are strung on beading wire)
- Scissors
- Beading needle (twisted wire)
- Hypo-cement glue (or clear nail polish)

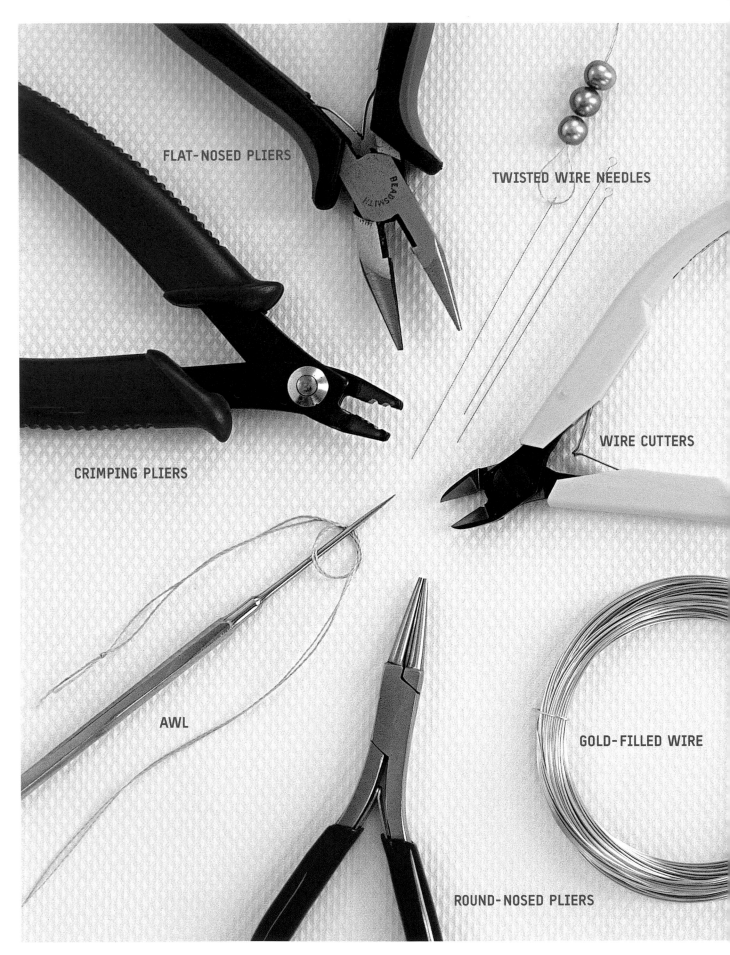

FLAT-NOSED PLIERS

TWISTED WIRE NEEDLES

CRIMPING PLIERS

WIRE CUTTERS

AWL

GOLD-FILLED WIRE

ROUND-NOSED PLIERS

FRENCH WIRE

SILK THREAD

BEADING WIRE

SILVER
CABLE CHAIN

GOLD-FILLED
CABLE CHAIN

DAISIES

Painstakingly constructed using a method called granulation, these are little silver or gold disks with tiny drops of the same metal applied around the edge. Used singly or in a group, they have a rich reflective texture that is delightful to the eye and to the touch.

CHARLOTTES

When these tiny glass beads are gold plated, they can be amazingly beautiful and provide a glittering string of light between the principal beads.

PLAIN ROUNDS

These are immensely versatile and can be used wherever a bigger bead needs to be emphasized, or at the beginning and end of strands to cover up beading wire and give a nice visual "tailing off" effect.

RONDELS

Like little doughnuts, these beads are made for embracing the sides of larger round beads. When set in between two rounds, they make a pleasing little band that gives a certain solidity to the design.

   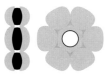

In practice, however, spacers tend to be fairly simple silver and gold beads, although they are sometimes more elaborate. For some designs, glass and glass crystal beads are used. Their most important characteristic is that they should emphasize rather than overwhelm the main beads. Spacers do not always do this by being restricted in number: sometimes they are used sparsely, while sometimes they comprise the majority of the design. Nor are they necessarily restricted in beauty. A whole strand of gold daisy spacers, for instance, can be a thing of pleasure. The spacers' position in the design determines their character. Spacers are beads that know when to hold back and let others take the central role.

STRINGING MATERIAL

The main structure of a neck "lace" is, by definition, a piece of thin material that can be wrapped like a lace around the neck. This material can be silk thread, leather thong, wire, chain, or one of the modern bead-stringing wires. Whatever the material, it must combine both strength and flexibility. Here are the stringing materials we recommend in *Simply Pearls*:

SILK THREAD

Silk is the traditional material for threading pearls. It is reasonably strong, easy to work with, and very supple. While modern beading wire is stronger and easier to use, no other material allows a strand of pearls to embrace the neck in quite the same way as silk. Threading beads onto silk with a beading needle of twisted wire is easy, but some makers now provide lengths of silk thread with a stiffened end that acts as its own needle and can then be cut off.

Silk also has some distinct disadvantages. It breaks if it is roughly handled, it stretches over time, and it gets dirty. Because of this, any pearls strung on silk will have to be restrung periodically, depending on how much they are worn. A good rule of thumb is that pearls that are worn regularly should be restrung every year or two.

Silk thread comes in several thicknesses, which are expressed by an arcane alphabetical code. The thickest silk thread is size FFF, while the thinnest is size 00. For all our projects, we will keep things simple and just use size F.

BEADING WIRE

Modern technology has tried to overcome the disadvantages of silk while still retaining its flexibility and ease of use. Beading wire, a relatively new and sophisticated product, is the closest thing to silk the technology has produced. Beading wire seems simple: it's just a few twisted strands of wire coated in plastic. But early attempts to create it were frustrating. The wire was too stiff to lie around the neck gracefully. It kinked when bent sharply and broke if mishandled. These problems were solved by twisting more and more strands of thinner wire to add both flexibility and strength. Today's 19- and 49-strand beading wires are increasingly kink resistant. They don't break under normal use, and although still not quite as supple as silk, they are very flexible. The thickness of beading wire is measured in inches despite the fact that the holes in beads are measured in millimeters. Again, to keep things simple, we recommend just one kind of beading wire for our designs: the best quality 49-strand size .015.

CHAIN

There are many different styles of chain, but we will only use two for the projects in *Simply Pearls*: cable chain and long and short chain.

SILK TIP
AFTER THREADING YOUR NEEDLE, RUN THE SILK ACROSS A BLOCK OF BEESWAX. THIS WILL KEEP THE THREAD TOGETHER AND HELP PREVENT FRAYING.

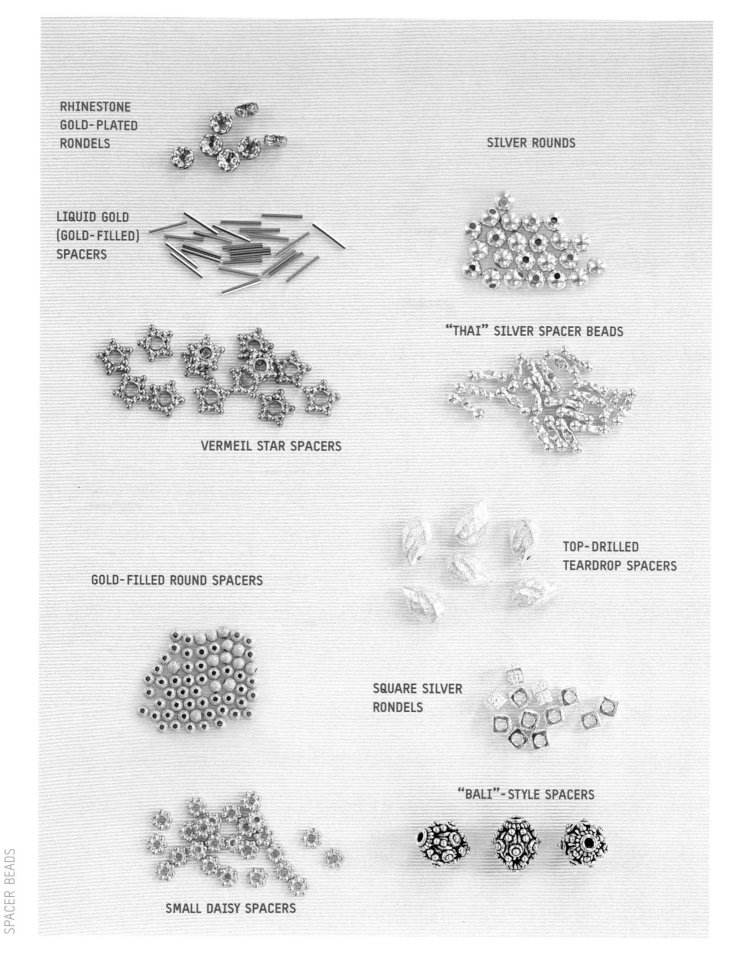

RHINESTONE
GOLD-PLATED
RONDELS

SILVER ROUNDS

LIQUID GOLD
(GOLD-FILLED)
SPACERS

"THAI" SILVER SPACER BEADS

VERMEIL STAR SPACERS

TOP-DRILLED
TEARDROP SPACERS

GOLD-FILLED ROUND SPACERS

SQUARE SILVER
RONDELS

"BALI"-STYLE SPACERS

SMALL DAISY SPACERS

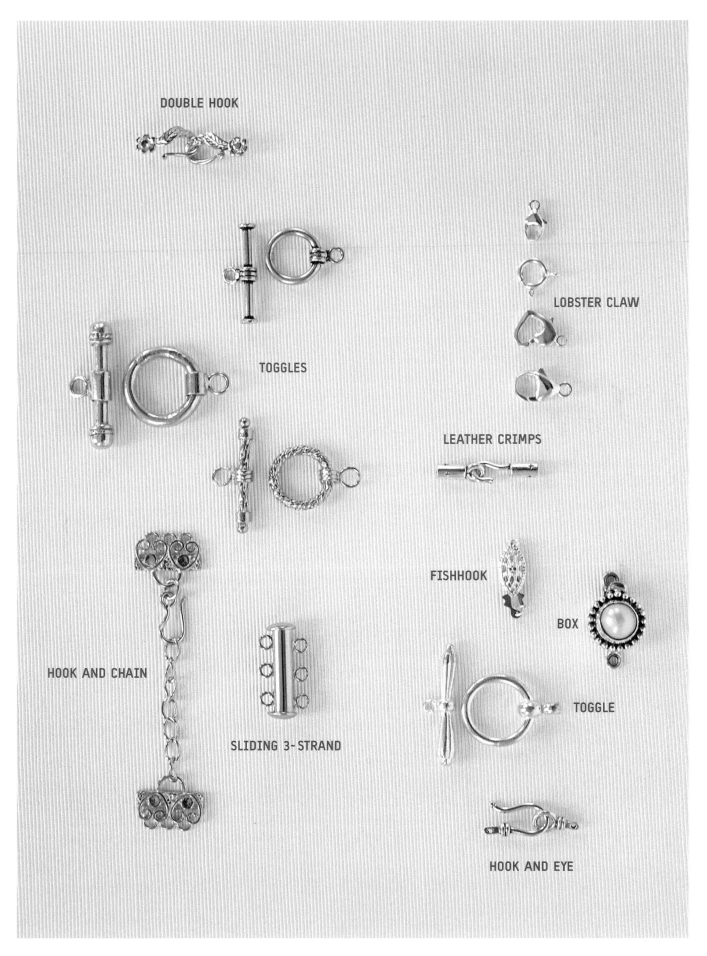

DOUBLE HOOK

LOBSTER CLAW

TOGGLES

LEATHER CRIMPS

FISHHOOK

BOX

HOOK AND CHAIN

SLIDING 3-STRAND

TOGGLE

HOOK AND EYE

I recommend that you use only sterling silver and gold-filled chain. Plated chain is cheaper, but it deteriorates quickly and is not an appropriate material to use with pearls. Solid gold chain is, of course, nice to have, but it's also very expensive. In appearance and durability, gold-filled chain is the next best thing.

WIRE

Stringing beads together with wire is easier than it first appears. In these designs we use just two types: sterling silver and gold-filled, both in a "half-hard" density. Wire is sold in another traditional measurement called "gauge." The wires used in these designs are either 22-, 24-, or 26-gauge, corresponding to .025, .020, and .016 of an inch.

FINDINGS FOR NECKLACES

These linking pieces are the jewelry maker's essential hardware. Just as the carpenter fills his toolbox with the nails, screws, and bolts needed to construct his works, the jeweler has her stock of clasps, wires, and links. There are many hundreds of different findings, but you need know only a few to make the jewelry in *Simply Pearls*. Most findings come in different metals and you should always use the one that is appropriate to the design. The basic materials, in order of cost and/or quality, are listed on page 23.

BEAD TIPS

Bead tips attach the end of a necklace thread to the clasp. The tip is designed to grip onto the knot you make after stringing the last bead, and comes in two varieties, the basket bead tip and the clamshell. The former works by trapping the knot in a little basket, while the latter sandwiches the knot between two concave wings that look like clamshells.

CRIMPS

Crimps are tiny metal beads that can be crushed flat with pliers. Beading wire is first threaded through the bead crimp, then through the loop of a clasp, and then back through the crimp. Finally, the little crimp is firmly but carefully squashed to attach the wire to the clasp. There is even a specialty tool, crimping pliers, that helps exert the right amount of pressure to make a perfect seal. You can also close crimps with simple flat-nosed pliers. Leather and cord crimps are even easier to use—just slip them over the end of the cord and squeeze to create a finished end.

CLASPS

Clasps for necklaces and bracelets come in a staggering variety. Several different methods are used to attach the two halves of a clasp, but all the styles are attached to the necklace pretty much the same way.

FRENCH WIRE AND CRIMP COVERS

These are clever ways of disguising the messy part of the necklace between the clasp and the first and last beads. French wire is a delicate coil of metal that looks like a miniature slinky toy and hides the whole length of thread beneath it. Crimp covers are hollow beads that cover a flattened crimp bead. While neither of these findings is necessary to make a necklace, they can add an extra touch of sophistication to your design.

FINDINGS FOR EARRINGS AND/OR NECKLACES

EARWIRES

Earrings for pierced ears use earwires designed to fit through the pierced hole. Other earrings use earwires that clamp on to the earlobe with a clip or a screw. Earwires for pierced ears should always be of good quality and made from material that will not cause an allergic reaction.

HEADPINS AND EYEPINS

These are simple pieces of straight wire on which you thread your beads. The "head" or "eye" at one end keeps the beads from falling off, and the other end is attached to the beading wire, chain, or earwire.

JUMP RINGS, SPLIT RINGS, AND PLAIN RINGS

These findings are often used for linking parts of necklaces and earrings. A jump ring is a simple metal loop that can be opened and closed by twisting. A split ring cannot be opened, but the item to be connected can be slipped onto it by feeding the item around the split in the side of the ring. (Split rings are just miniature versions of the metal rings on key chains.) A plain ring is one that cannot be opened, as the ends are soldered together.

STYLES OF CLASPS

- Hook and eye
- Fish hook
- Box
- Toggle
- Lobster claw
- Spring ring
- Sliding

FINDINGS MATERIALS
GOLD
Use only with pearls of high value.

GOLD-FILLED
Use with any good pearls.

VERMEIL (sterling silver plated with gold)
Use with modest value pearls or faux pearls.

NIOBIUM (hypo-allergenic metal)
Use if you have an allergic reaction to silver.

SILVER (sterling or better)
Use with any real pearls.

PLATED BASE METAL
Use only with the very cheapest pearls and faux pearls.

THE QUALITIES OF PEARLS

PEARLS COME IN MANY DIFFERENT SHAPES, COLORS, QUALITIES, AND PRICES. WHILE THERE IS GENERALLY COMMON AGREEMENT ON WHAT MAKES A TRULY VALUABLE PEARL, PERCEPTION OF BEAUTY IS VERY MUCH IN THE EYE OF THE BEHOLDER. ALL PEARLS HAVE MERIT WHEN USED IN THE RIGHT DESIGN.

Although there is no universal system of grading pearls, there is a consensus on what aspects of the gem creates part of its value. The following sections describe the qualities by which pearls are judged.

SHAPE

Some pearl shapes, such as mabes and blister pearls, are formed on the shell itself, which is then cut to make flat-backed that can be set in silver or gold. In this book, however, "pearls" means drilled pearls, or pearl beads. Throughout the ages it has been so usual to drill and string pearls that several languages use the same word for both pearls and beads. If you are looking for any beads in France, you ask for perles and for perlen in Germany.

LUSTER

Luster is the most important of the light effects caused by the structure of a pearl. Rather than just a surface reflection, luster is the warm glow that seems to come from within a pearl. Because nacre is translucent, some of the light falling on a pearl travels though one or more layers before being reflected back to the eye. This creates the effect of depth; the stronger this effect, the more a given pearl is valued. When all other qualities are similar, the luster of the pearl determines its price.

COLOR

Although people think of pearls as creamy white, they often come in wonderfully subtle colors ranging from yellow and gold to pink, blue, green, and purple. The value of any particular color is dependent on fashion and scarcity. Pearls are described as having three types of color: body color (the pearl's basic color), overtone, and an optical effect called orient.

BASIC PEARL BEAD SHAPES

- Spherical: Round and near round
- Symmetrical: Oval, button, drop, potato, rice, and baroque
- Keshi
- Faceted
- Other shapes: stick, coin cross, bar, "cornflakes"

Some pearls display a translucent surface color, or overtone, that subtly alters the nature of the body color. One of the most beautiful qualities of pearls is "orient," an iridescent effect similar to the rainbow of colors you might see on the surface of a soap bubble or an oil slick.

SURFACE QUALITY

Since pearls are organic, a perfectly even, flawless surface is astonishingly rare. Instead, just like the people who wear them, these gems are afflicted with a variety of spots, bumps, and wrinkles. Although in certain cases a lot of bumps or wrinkles may add some character, it is generally considered in a pearl (as in people) that the fewer of these blemishes, the better. Pearl producers will try and limit these surface blemishes as much as possible. For instance, if a single spot mars a beautiful round pearl, you can be certain that the seller will drill the hole through it. You can be sure that your pearls will contain some surface irregularities. If these are few and minor, they are considered acceptable within the various gradations of value. If the flaws are large or serious, such as chips or cracks, they will greatly reduce the value of the pearl.

SIZE

"The bigger, the better" is the general rule when it comes to pearls, although it would be far more accurate to say, "The bigger, the more expensive." Pearls are usually sized to the nearest half millimeter. Spherical pearls normally vary from 2 millimeters to 20 millimeters in diameter, and cost can increase dramatically in the larger sizes. The increase in cost is not necessarily consistent, however, and it varies among the different pearl varieties. Size cost is often affected by the popularity of the size and the quantities available. So while there might be a very small difference between a 6-millimeter and a 6.5-millimeter pearl, there could be a far greater difference between a 7.5 millimeter and an 8 millimeter pearl.

Traditionally, women have hoped that as they grow older, they will acquire bigger and bigger pearls. While a young woman might be thrilled with a strand of 6 millimeter pearls, a matron of mature years is more likely to be thinking about 8 millimeters and up. There have to be some benefits of aging! In the contemporary world of fashion, however, there is a place for all sizes, and stunning jewelry can be composed from even the tiniest of pearls. "Beautiful" is always better than "big" (although the matron in me thinks that "big and beautiful" has a pleasant sound when it comes to pearls!).

MATCHING

With strands of natural pearls, matched sets are considerably more valuable than the sum of their individual parts. Since pearls are produced in a biological process, no two are ever identical. Producing a strand of large pearls of the same quality and of the same size or in perfectly graduated order used to be a matter of collecting them over months or even years before finding exactly the sizes needed. Things are a lot easier with cultured pearls since the producers can start with a nucleus bead ground to just the right size. Still, there is no guarantee that any two pearls will come out looking the same. It takes patience and effort to sort even cultured pearls into strands of the same size, color, and quality. Strands of pearls fetch a premium for the uniformity of their size and appearance.

JUST

PEARLS

MAKING PEARL JEWELRY

Making necklaces and earrings is simplicity itself. Although you still have to turn to a professional jeweler for setting rings and casting metals, you can master the basic techniques of stringing beads and bending wire in an evening. Combine these simple skills with a few inexpensive tools, add the basic ingredients of beads and findings, and you are ready to start making your own jewelry. Don't be intimidated! Compared to preparing a decent meal, making a piece of jewelry is child's play—it not only takes fewer tools, but also leaves no dishes to wash up!

Every necklace or pair of earrings begins with a design. While it is perfectly possible to throw random beads on a string, it's very unlikely that the results will be satisfying. My approach to jewelry design begins with a simple premise: "The purpose of any body decoration is to enhance the look of the wearer." I care, therefore, that the design will go well with the wearer's face as well as with her clothes, her mood, and the impression she wishes to make. Some designers might disagree and view the body as a convenient frame for exhibiting an interesting object. If you are making jewelry for yourself, however, you will probably be more sympathetic to the view that the jewels are there to make you look good—not the other way around.

While the jewelry designs in this book are in every way contemporary, they are integrated with classic styles and materials that consistently return to the forefront of fashion and that have a proven record of making their owners feel they are wearing the "right stuff."

Although you can follow the project instructions and replicate the jewelry in this book as shown in the photographs, do not be reluctant to experiment and add your own touches. You should think of the instructions as recipes in which even small changes of ingredients can create a different but delightful flavor. Whether through desire for variation or a simple lack of access to the precise ingredients, you should not be afraid to substitute and create your own unique "dish." Making these designs will, after all, be even more rewarding if they include a dash of your own good judgment.

When designing with pearls, this sense of individual creativity is sort of forced upon us anyway. Because pearls are all slightly different, the very act of combining them will make your creations unique. Unless they are faux, none of the pearls you buy will be exactly the same as those photographed in this book. This natural and pleasant uniqueness of pearls will make each one of these designs truly your own, even if you follow the recipe as closely as possible.

It is my hope that after you have made a few of the projects in this book, you will use your skills and your own design sense to introduce variations and then to start creating entirely new designs of your own.

HOW TO CREATE YOUR OWN DESIGNS

Whether substituting ingredients or planning a whole new design, you should follow these basic guidelines:

1. Do not mix inappropriate materials. While it is obvious that you would not use real pearls with plastic beads, other combinations are less obvious no-nos. In case you are not yet ready to trust your own eye, chapter 3, "Designing with Pearls," includes suggestions for gems and other materials that mix beautifully with pearls.

2. Never use materials that look cheap, no matter what they actually cost. They will make the good look bad.

3. Use materials that will be in fashion for decades rather than for weeks. Today's fad is toast tomorrow.

Before you attempt any of the projects in this book, you will need to read the instructions for basic jewelry-making in chapter 4, "Jewelry Techniques." This chapter contains information on knotting and stringing, making continuous strands, attaching clasps, wrapping wire, measuring, and using essential tools. Read chapter 4 carefully, but note that these techniques are best learned through actual practice. When you feel comfortable, jump in and get started. As with all crafts, the only way to master the art of jewelry making is by actually doing it.

DESIGNING FOR YOU

When you are making jewelry for yourself or for friends and family, you have the opportunity to create something that is truly customized. Try matching the colors with favorite clothes, skin and hair tones, or other preferences. Also consider size. Bigger necks and busts obviously call for longer necklaces, but the actual bead size can be just as important. In designing commissioned pieces, I always first consider the shape of the client—the more delicate her bone structure, the more delicate the jewelry.

While fashion and mood will dictate overall bead sizes, the general rule "bigger women need bigger beads" is a good one to follow. There are always exceptions, but size in jewelry is as important as size in clothing. No piece should overwhelm or be overwhelmed by the body it adorns. In jewelry design, the goal is harmony, not competition.

THE SIMPLE STRAND OF GRADUATED PEARLS

THE SIMPLE STRAND OF PEARLS IS AT THE HEART OF EVERY WOMAN'S JEWELRY COLLECTION. BEFORE TRYING THESE FOUR DESIGNS, REFER TO "GETTING KNOTTED" (PAGE 114) AND THEN PRACTICE YOUR SKILLS WITH A FEW GLASS BEADS. WHEN YOU TRY MAKING YOUR FIRST SIMPLE PEARL STRAND, DON'T BE NERVOUS—THE WORST THAT COULD HAPPEN IS THAT YOU MIGHT HAVE TO CUT THE THREAD AND START OVER AGAIN.

1.
SWEET SIXTEEN NECKLACE

14-INCH CHOKER, PERFECT FOR THAT FIRST REAL STRAND OF PEARLS

Follow the instructions for knotting on silk (page 114) and using basket bead tips (page 118). Attach one part of the clasp. Knot on enough beads to make about 13 inches of length, and try the strand around your neck. Remember to allow for the length of the clasp. Knot on a few more pearls as necessary to get the right length. Try it again. Attach the bead tip, keeping everything nice and snug. Put on the other half of the clasp. Voila!

TOOLS
Beading Needle, Awl, Scissors

MATERIALS
- 65   4.5mm round light cream-colored pearls (about four-fifths of a 16" strand)
- 2   gold-filled basket bead tips
- 1   gold-filled box clasp, 10mm long
- 2   yds of size F silk

2.
THE CLASSIC

WHAT EVERY WOMAN NEEDS

Follow the instructions for stringing on silk (page 114) and using French wire (page 120). Attach one part of the clasp. Knot on enough beads to make about 15 inches of length, and try the strand around your neck. Knot on a few more pearls as necessary to get the right length, keeping in mind that your last three beads will only be knotted after attaching the French wire. Attach the other half of the clasp using the rest of the French wire.

TOOLS
Beading Needle, Awl, Scissors

MATERIALS
- 54   7mm round white freshwater pearls (a little less than a 16" strand)
- 2 $\frac{1}{4}$"   pieces of silver French wire
- 1   sterling silver box clasp (shown here with a mabe pearl)
- 2   yds of size F silk

3.
BIG-GIRL PEARLS

WHAT EVERY WOMAN WANTS

Follow the instructions for stringing on silk (page 114) and using clamshell bead tips (page 116). Attach one part of the clasp. Knot on enough beads to make about 15 inches of length, and try the strand around your neck. Remember to allow for the length of the clasp. Knot on a few more pearls as necessary to get the right length. Try it again, and then add the other half of the clasp.

TOOLS
Beading Needle, Awl, Flat-Nosed Pliers, Scissors

MATERIALS
42   9mm round cream Akoya pearls
      (a little less than a 16" strand)

 2   gold-filled clamshell bead tips

 1   gold hook-and-eye clasp 20mm long

 2   yds of size F silk

4.
FABULOUS FAUX

A CHANEL-STYLE ROPE

What could be easier? No clasps, no bead tips, just silk thread. Tie a knot at the end of your doubled thread leaving a good long tail (about 6 inches). Now follow the instructions for making a continuous strand (page 122).

TOOLS
Beading Needle, Awl, Scissors

MATERIALS
For a 32" opera length strand (for rope length, simply add another strand of faux pearls):

76   10mm round cream Swarovski faux pearls
      (two 16" strands, with four pearls left
      over to make earrings)

 4   yds of size F silk

NOTE
Faux (French for "fake") pearls were widely used by the French couturiere Coco Chanel, who helped them become classic accessories.

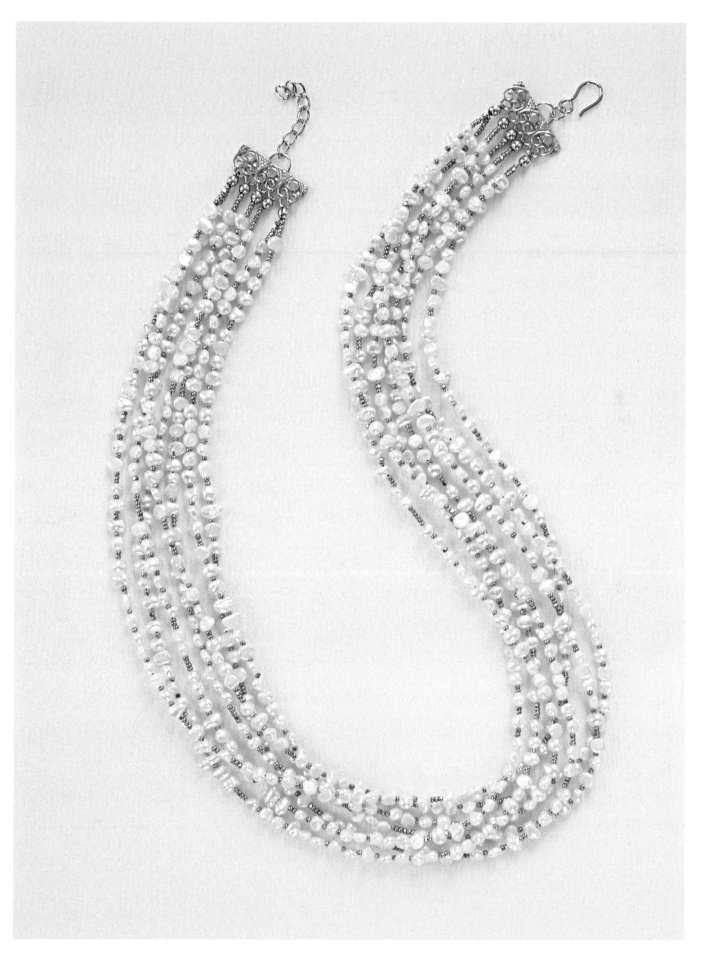

5.
THE CLASSIC THREE-STRAND NECKLACE

THIS STYLE WAS A FAMOUS FAVORITE OF JACQUELINE KENNEDY ONASSIS. TO MAKE IT, YOU MUST BE CAREFUL TO GET EACH OF THE THREE STRANDS THE CORRECT LENGTH. THE SECOND AND THIRD STRANDS MUST HAVE MORE PEARLS THAN THE FIRST SO THAT THE THREE LIE PARALLEL TO ONE ANOTHER AND DON'T OVERLAP WHEN ATTACHED TO THE CLASP.

1. Make the first knotted strand, using enough beads to make about 14 inches of length (see "Getting Knotted," page 114). This particular clasp adds more than an inch to the overall length of the necklace. If you choose another clasp that adds less, you can increase the length of the pearl strand. Using the bead tip, attach one end of the strand to the top row of one side of the clasp. Try it around your neck to see if it is long enough. If it is the right length, finish it off with a basket bead tip and attach it to the top row of the other half of the clasp.

2. Make the second knotted strand a bit longer than the first, with two more pearls than you used on the first strand. Attach one end of the strand to the middle row of the clasp. Try the necklace on. If you hold the knot of the last pearl to the ring of the clasp, the two rows should just touch. If the second strand overlaps the first, add another bead (or more) until the strands form two parallel lines. When the length is right, use a bead tip to finish off, and attach the end to the middle row of the other part of the clasp.

3. Make the third knotted strand a bit longer than the second, with one more pearl than you used on the second one. Attach one end of the strand to the third row of the clasp. Try the necklace on, holding the knot of the last pearl to the ring of the clasp. The rows should just touch. If they overlap, add another pearl (or more) until the rows form three parallel lines. When the length is right, use a bead tip to finish off the strand, and attach it to the third row of the other part of the clasp.

TOOLS
Beading Needle, Awl, Scissors

MATERIALS
3 16" strands of semi-baroque 8mm Akoya pearls. (You will have some pearls left over, possibly enough for a bracelet and definitely plenty for matching earrings.)

1 sterling silver 3-row clasp set with marcasite (a metallic gemstone)

8 yds of size F white silk thread

6 sterling silver basket-bead tips

NOTE
Test the length of each strand around your neck before you attach it to the clasp to be sure it doesn't overlap the others or create a large gap between them. Since the pearl sizes will vary a bit, this measuring method is the only way to be sure to get the three strands the proper length.

6.
MULTISTRAND KESHI PEARL NECKLACE

THIS NECKLACE IS DESIGNED SO THAT THE STRANDS OF PEARLS OVERLAP AND CLUSTER TOGETHER. IT COMBINES SMALL KESHI PEARLS, WHICH CAN BE FAIRLY INEXPENSIVE, WITH TINY GOLD-PLATED CHARLOTTE SEED BEADS FOR A STUNNING EFFECT. THE PATTERN IS QUITE RANDOM; USE YOUR OWN JUDGMENT ABOUT HOW TO MIX BEADS, OR SEE THE PHOTO ON PAGE 35.

1. To get seven strands onto a five-row clasp, the two outside rows are doubled. To make one of these doubled strands, start with 42 inches of beading wire. Fold it in half. Pass the folded V-shape end of the wire through a crimp and attach to the top loop of one side of the clasp. Now string on your charlottes and pearls until the strand is 16 inches long. Put tape around the end of the beading wire to keep the beads from falling off. Fill the other side of the doubled wire with charlottes and pearls. Make the strand 16$\frac{1}{4}$ inches long. Holding the two wire ends so that the beads can't fall off, remove the tape and insert both ends into a crimp bead. Bring the wire through the top loop of the other half of the clasp and back through the crimp. Before you squeeze the crimp shut, adjust the wires so the beads are snug with no gaps between them. The first wire will be a bit shorter than the second, so tighten them accordingly.

2. To make the third strand, cut 20 inches of beading wire. Attach one end to the second row of the clasp and fill it with pearls and charlottes to a length of 16$\frac{1}{2}$ inches. Make sure the beads are snug, and attach it to the next row of the clasp. Repeat this for the fourth strand, increasing the length of pearls and charlottes to 16$\frac{3}{4}$ inches, and attaching the fourth strand to the middle row of the clasp. Repeat for the fifth strand, attaching it to the fourth row of the clasp to make a length of 17 inches.

3. Make the sixth and seventh strands using the doubled-wire technique. The first line of this doubled strand should have 17$\frac{1}{4}$ inches of pearls and charlottes, and the second 17$\frac{1}{2}$ inches. The longer length goes at the bottom of your necklace.

TOOLS
Wire Cutters, Crimping Pliers

MATERIALS

- 5   16" strands of small side-drilled keshi pearls in the 3–4mm size range
- 3   20" strands (or 5 grams) of gold-plated charlotte beads, size 13/0. **Charlottes are little glass beads that have an irregular cut on one side and are then gold plated**
- 10   gold-filled crimp beads
- 10   gold-filled crimp bead covers
- 13   ft of .015 49-strand beading wire

7.
RICH GIRL'S PEARLS

THIS RECIPE IS NOT FOR THE FAINT OF HEART. TO FILL THIS NECKLACE WITH GRADUATED TAHITIAN BLACK PEARLS, YOU WILL HAVE TO SAVE UP YOUR MONEY (UNLESS YOU HAVE A LOT OF DISPOSABLE INCOME). JUST REMEMBER, THOUGH, THAT A SIMILAR DESIGN IN THE JEWELER'S WINDOW PRICED FOR TENS OF THOUSANDS OF DOLLARS CAN BE YOURS IF YOU MAKE IT YOURSELF FOR, WELL, JUST A FEW THOUSAND.

SIMPLY STUNNING STRANDS OF PEARLS

FOR THESE "INVESTMENT-GRADE" DESIGNS, YOU'LL NEED STRANDS OF REALLY BEAUTIFUL PEARLS. IF YOU CAN'T AFFORD A MATCHED SET OF PERFECTLY ROUND SOUTH SEA PEARLS IN THE 14-MILLIMETER RANGE, BAROQUE PEARLS ARE THE ANSWER. THEIR IRREGULAR ROUNDISH SHAPE IS AS UNIQUE AND INTERESTING AS THAT OF CONSISTENT ROUND PEARLS.

1. Lay out your pearls in a line and arrange them in graduated order so that the largest is in the center and the smallest are at the ends. Refer to the instructions for stringing on silk thread (page 114) and for using French wire to attach clasps (page 120).

2. Because you're working with French wire, the first pearl on your thread will be the third from the end on the finished necklace (see page 120). So, at the end of the graduated line of pearls at which you are going to start stringing, switch the first and the third pearls.

3. String the pearls following the instructions for stringing on silk thread. Take your time to make sure the quality of the knotting matches the quality of your pearls. Be sure that the strand fits around your neck properly before finishing it off.

4. Attach the clasp using the instructions for using French wire on page 120. Enjoy!

RICH GIRL'S PEARLS, VARIATION

Follow the instructions for the preceding design, but substitute silver-gray Baroque pearls and the other "Variation" ingredients listed at right.

GRADUATED PEARLS
WHEN YOU SEE THE COST OF REALLY LARGE PEARLS, YOU START TO WONDER WHETHER THE ONES AT THE BACK OF YOUR NECKLACE NEED TO BE QUITE AS BIG AS THE ONES IN FRONT! THE ANSWER IS A GRADUATED STRAND: THE BIGGEST PEARLS FALL AT THE CENTER OF THE NECKLACE, AND AS THEY GO BACK AROUND YOUR NECK AND OUT OF SIGHT, THEY BECOME SMALLER. THE STYLE CREATES A PLEASING PERSPECTIVE AND LETS YOU SAVE A LITTLE CASH. THE DESIGNS ON THESE TWO PAGES ARE GRADUATED.

TOOLS
Beading Needle, Awl, Scissors

MATERIALS
- 30   baroque Tahitian black pearls, graduated in size from 10–15mm (a 16" strand, with a couple of pearls left over for earrings.)
- ½"   silver French wire
- 1   round 10mm box clasp, brushed white gold with tiny diamonds.
- 2   yds of size F black silk

FOR RICH GIRL'S PEARLS VARIATION
- 30   silver-gray baroque South Sea pearls graduated from 10–15mm (a full 16" strand)
- 1   round 11mm box clasp, granulated white gold with tiny diamonds
- 2   yds of size F white silk

8.
FLOATING PEARLS NECKLACE

SOMETIMES KNOWN AS SCATTERED PEARLS, THE "FLOATING" PEARLS IN THIS NECKLACE ACHIEVE A REMARKABLY LIGHT AND DELICATE LOOK, WHILE THE DESIGN MAKES ECONOMICAL USE OF ITS INGREDIENTS. I CHOSE NEAR-ROUND 7-MILLIMETER FRESHWATER PEARLS, BUT FEEL FREE TO SUBSTITUTE THEM WITH THE PEARLS OF YOUR CHOICE (SEE NOTE BELOW).

1. Thread a beading needle and make a knot at one end of the thread. (Note that this is one of the few silk thread designs in which you do not double your thread. A single thread is used.) Attach the bead tip (see page 116). Measure ³/₈ inch from the bead tip and make a knot. Use your awl to make sure that the knot is in the right position (see page 117). Now add a charlotte, a daisy spacer, a pearl, a daisy spacer, and a charlotte.

2. Make another knot, using your awl to make sure that the beads are tightly held between the two knots. Measure another ³/₈ inch of thread from that knot and make another. Repeat pattern of charlotte, spacer, pearl, spacer, charlotte, knot, ³/₈ inch of thread, until you have used all 16 pearls.

3. After the last pearl/spacer group, add the ending bead tip. Attach the toggle clasp to the bead tips.

TOOLS
Beading Needle, Awl, Scissors

MATERIALS
- 16 7mm round, near round or potato pearls
- 32 3.5mm gold-filled or vermeil daisy spacers
- 32 gold charlottes
- 2 gold-filled basket bead tips
- 1 vermeil toggle clasp
- 2 ft of beige or light-pink silk thread, size F

NOTE
The effect of this subtle style depends on achieving the right balance between the pearls and the thread-filled spaces. If your pearls are too small, they will make no impact; If they are too large, they will overwhelm the thread. Pearls between 6mm and 8mm seem to work best.

9.
SINGLE-STRAND NECKLACE

THIS DESIGN USES TOP-DRILLED TEARDROP PEARLS TO CREATE
A "BIGGER" LOOK—ARRANGING THESE PEARLS SO THAT THEY
FALL ON OPPOSITE SIDES OF THE SINGLE-STRAND THREAD GIVES
EACH TRIO OF SMALL PEARLS THE SAME EFFECT AS A SINGLE
LARGE PEARL.

1. Start the necklace by threading on a crimp. Pass the beading
   wire through the ring of one clasp back through the crimp.
   Tighten the beading wire around the ring, and squeeze the
   crimp shut. Add three silver beads to cover the tail of the
   beading wire and cut. Add the gemstone or crystal bead.

2. Now thread on three teardrop pearls and one potato pearl.
   Repeat this pattern 19 times or until the necklace is the length
   you wish. (Remember to try it on to make sure.)

3. Add a final set of three teardrop pearls, then the other rondel,
   the three silver beads, and the crimping bead. Bring the beading
   wire through the ring of the other side of the clasp and back
   through the crimp and silver beads. **BEFORE YOU FINISH OFF
   THE NECKLACE BY CLOSING THE CRIMP, MAKE SURE THAT
   ALL THE TEARDROP PEARLS ARE ARRANGED SO THAT THE
   MIDDLE PEARL IN EACH TRIO IS ON THE OPPOSITE SIDE OF
   THE OTHER TWO.** Now tighten the necklace so there are no
   spaces between the beads, close the crimp, and snip off any
   remaining beading wire.

TOOLS
Wire Cutters, Crimping Pliers

MATERIALS

19	8–9mm dyed blue freshwater potato-shaped pearls (a little less than half a 16" strand)
60	5 by 6mm dyed green top-drilled teardrop pearls (about half a 16" strand)
2	4mm faceted blue rondel gemstone or Swarovski crystal beads
6	2.5mm sterling silver round beads
2	sterling silver crimp beads
1	sterling silver toggle clasp
20"	beading wire

10.
DOUBLE-STRAND NECKLACE

FEEL FREE TO VARY THE RANDOM PATTERN OF PEARLS AND CRYSTALS IN THIS NECKLACE TO SUIT YOUR OWN SENSE OF SYMMETRY. DOUBLE AB-COATED CRYSTALS HAVE AN IRIDESCENT FINISH ("AB" STANDS FOR AURORA BOREALIS) THAT GIVES THE NECKLACE REFLECTIONS. IF YOU USE DIFFERENT COLORS OF PEARLS, USE CRYSTAL BEADS THAT MATCH THEM.

1. Cut the beading wire into two equal lengths. Start the first strand by threading on a crimp bead. Pass the beading wire through the loop of the clasp and back through the crimp. Tighten the wire around the loop and close the crimp. Add the two gold beads and the crystal bead to cover the tail of the wire. Snip off any of the tail that protrudes from the crystal bead. Then, string a series of beads as follows: 1 gold bead, 2 green pearls, 1 crystal, 5 pearls, 1 crystal, 13 pearls, 1 crystal, 3 pearls, 1 crystal, 8 pearls, 1 crystal, 9 pearls, 1 crystal, 8 pearls, 1 crystal, 6 pearls, 1 crystal, 1 pearl, 1 crystal, 10 pearls, 1 crystal, 8 pearls, 1 crystal, 5 pearls, 1 crystal, 11 pearls, 1 crystal. The pearls should fit snugly together, each facing opposite its neighbor. Check the length around your neck, remembering that the strand will get shorter when you twist it. Add enough pearls to achieve the necessary length (the distance from pearl to pearl should be about 16 inches). Then add 1 gold bead, 1 crystal, 2 gold beads, and a crimp. Finish the strand by attaching it to the loop of the other side of the clasp.

2. Make the second strand the same way as the first, but at each end, use a pattern of 1 gold bead, 1 crystal, then 2 gold beads. Try to arrange the crystal beads so they do not lie exactly opposite those on the first strand. The number of pearls, starting from the same side as the first strand, is as follows: 2, 4, 5, 3, 5, 6, 6, 7, 1, 6, 5, 3, 6, 5, 5, 2, 5, 3. Adjust the final number of pearls so that the second strand is approximately the same length as the first. Attach the finished second strand to the clasp. Attach the crimp covers to all the crimps. To wear, twist the necklace a few times until you achieve a look that pleases you.

TOOLS
Wire Cutters, Crimping Pliers

MATERIALS

1	16" strand of 5 by 6mm dyed green top-drilled teardrop pearls
1	16" strand of 6 by 8mm dyed light blue top-drilled teardrop pearls
34	4mm double AB-coated light sapphire Swarovski bicone crystal beads
12	gold-filled 3.5mm round beads
4	gold-filled crimp beads
4	gold-filled crimp bead covers
40"	beading wire
1	large (17mm) vermeil toggle clasp

NOTE:
When a double strand is twisted, it becomes shorter. Although the overall length of this design is almost 18 inches, when twisted, it is a standard short length.

If the teardrop pearls are arranged tightly on the strands, they will fall naturally to opposite sides.

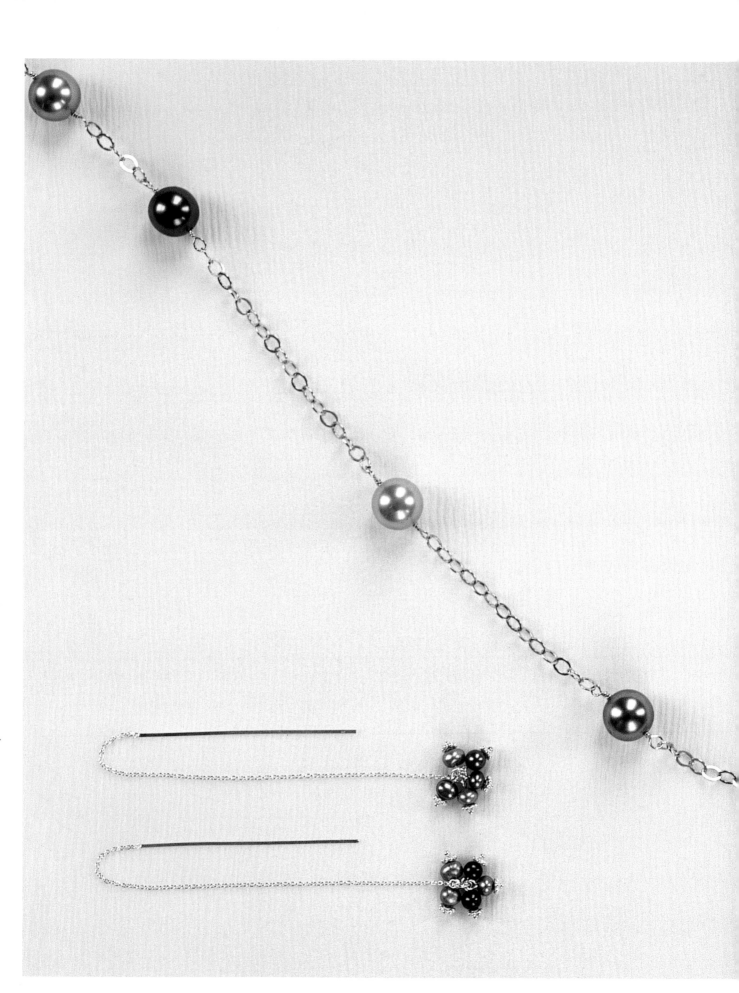

11.
FAUX PEARLS WITH CHAIN

THE SEEMINGLY RANDOM DESIGN OF THIS OPERA-LENGTH NECKLACE COMBINES PEARLS IN MIXED COLORS WITH VARYING LENGTHS OF CHAIN BETWEEN THE PEARLS. FEEL FREE TO MIX COLORS, LENGTHS, OR OTHER PEARLS TO EXPRESS YOUR DESIGN IDEAS. THESE LARGE FAUX PEARLS CREATE QUITE AN IMPACT.

WORKING WITH CHAIN
CHAIN SERVES TWO PURPOSES IN JEWELRY-MAKING. IT IS THE PRACTICAL HARDWARE THAT STRINGS THE BEADS TOGETHER AS WELL AS AN ESSENTIAL VISUAL ELEMENT OF THE DESIGN. THERE ARE A MULTITUDE OF DIFFERENT TYPES OF CHAIN AND MANY WAYS THEY CAN BE USED. HERE ARE A ROPE, A LARIAT, AND EARRINGS THAT EXPRESS SOME OF THAT VARIETY.

1. Refer to the instructions on wire wrapping (page 127) to learn how to make a wire-wrapped loop. Start by cutting the 24-gauge wire into fourteen 2-inch lengths.

2. With your round-nosed pliers, grip a 2-inch piece of wire approximately $1/2$ inch from the end. Bend the wire to form a loop, but do not wrap the wire yet. Note carefully where the wire is gripped between your pliers. Every loop must be the same size, so you must put the wire in the same spot in the pliers every time you make a loop. Mark the spot on the pliers with a felt-tip pen if you need a visual cue.

3. Cut a piece of chain approximately $3/4$ inch long. Slip the loop onto an end link of the chain, and finish wrapping it. Slip a silver-gray bead onto the wire, and make another half-formed loop at the other end. Now cut a piece of chain approximately 1-inch long and attach the end to the loop. Finish closing the loop.

4. Now repeat the procedure of making a loop and attaching it to the end of the chain. Add 1 blue pearl, then approximately 4 inches of chain; 1 green pearl and $3 1/4$ inches of chain; 1 brown pearl and 1 inch of chain; 1 dark-gray pearl and $3/4$ inch of chain; 1 silver-gray pearl and $4 1/4$ inch of chain; 1 blue-gray pearl and $2 1/2$ inches of chain; 1 dark-gray pearl and 4 inches of chain; 1 silver-gray pearl and $3/4$ inch of chain; 1 green pearl and 1 inch of chain; 1 blue pearl and $2 3/4$ inches of chain; 1 grey pearl and 3 inches of chain; and 1 green pearl and $3 3/4$ inch of chain. Finally, add a brown pearl and attach it to the other beginning end of the necklace.

TOOLS
Round-Nosed Pliers, Flat-Nosed Pliers, Wire Cutters

MATERIALS
- 14   12mm faux South Sea pearls in mixed colors (16" strand is best so that you can pick and choose the colors you like—the rest of the pearls can be used to create another necklace or earrings)
- 3   ft gold-filled flat cable chain with 6mm links
- 3   ft gold-filled 24-gauge wire (half-hard)

12.
LARIAT WITH CHAIN AND PEARL DROPS

ALTHOUGH THIS PARTICULAR NECKLACE LOOKS INTRICATE, THE 40 LITTLE MULTICOLORED PEARL DROPS ARE VERY EASY TO MAKE AND ATTACH TO THE CHAIN.

1. Start by making the 40 pearl drops. Choose pearls with colors that will look interesting together. Slip a daisy spacer bead and then a pearl onto the head pin (see page 126). Use round-nosed pliers to make a very small loop (about 2 to 3 millimeters), but do not close the loop all the way.

2. Attach three of the drops to the end link of the chain. Use your judgment to space out the colors along the chain. Then add 2 more drops on either side of the next link, 2 more to either side of the next, and so on.

3. When you've added all your pearl drops, attach the spring clasp to the other end of the chain, using the split ring to connect the final link to the clasp. To wear, loop the chain around your neck and attach the clasp to the link that lets the pearl cluster hang where you want it.

LARIAT
THIS STYLE ENABLES YOU TO CREATE A VERY LONG "CENTERPIECE" WHERE THE TAIL OF THE LARIAT HANGS DOWN. WITH A SPRING CLASP, YOU CAN FIX THE LARIAT AT VARIOUS LENGTHS ACCORDING TO THE LINK OF THE CHAIN ONTO WHICH IT IS HOOKED.

TOOLS

Round-Nosed Pliers, Flat-Nosed Pliers, Wire Cutters

MATERIALS

- 40 5mm dyed freshwater pearls in a variety of colors (about half a multicolored strand)
- 40 ¹/₂" sterling silver headpins with ball tip
- 40 4mm sterling silver daisy spacer beads
- 18" sterling silver cable chain with 5mm links
- 1 sterling silver spring clasp
- 1 4mm sterling silver split ring

13.
CHAIN EARRINGS WITH PEARL DROPS

THESE EARRINGS CAN BE WORN BY THEMSELVES OR MATCHED WITH THE LARIAT.

1. Make the 10 pearl drops as described in the instructions for the lariat. Close the loops all the way. Open a jump ring. Add five of the drops, making sure not to repeat any of the colors. Slip the jump ring through the end loop of the earwire and close. Add the other five drops to the other earwire in the same manner.

MATERIALS

- 10 5mm dyed freshwater pearls in a variety of colors (use some of the pearls from the other half of the strand you used for the lariat, and don't repeat any color more than once)
- 10 ¹/₂" sterling silver headpins with ball tip
- 10 4mm sterling silver daisy spacer beads
- 2 sterling silver post-and-chain earwires
- 2 4mm sterling silver jump rings

THE HISTORY
OF PEARLS

IT IS POINTLESS TO SPECULATE ON THE MOMENT WHEN THE FIRST
PEARL WAS USED AS A GEM. SINCE BEADS OF SHELL OR STONE DATE
FROM MORE THAN 40,000 YEARS AGO, WE CAN ASSUME THAT PEARLS
WERE USED AS BODY DECORATION FAR EARLIER THAN THE
BEGINNINGS OF RECORDED HISTORY.

One of the first written records is in a Chinese text of the twenty-third
century B.C. The writer somewhat critically observes that a tribute to his
king contains, "strings of pearls not quite round." Royal treasuries have
been major repositories of fine pearls ever since.

Ancient Indian, Middle Eastern, and European civilizations all placed
high value on pearls. Cleopatra is said to have dissolved a
priceless pearl in wine in order to demonstrate to Mark
Antony the limitless wealth of Egypt. The Romans adored
pearls. Indeed, the Roman historian Suetonius cites them as a motive for
Caesar's abortive invasion of Britain in 55 B.C., and the only trophy
Caesar is said to have displayed was a corselet made of British
freshwater pearls. That the rivers of Britain, a country Tacitus called
"objectionable with its frequent rains," could provide a source of fine
pearls must have been one of the few attractions the island offered to the
Romans.

Throughout most of history, the main saltwater sources of pearls were
the coasts of India, the Persian Gulf, the Red Sea, Burma, the Philippines,
and Japan. Freshwater pearls were gathered in China and northern
Europe. The constant depletion of these resources led to an enormous
increase in the value of pearls and strict controls on gathering. Large
round pearls became so rare and valuable that a single one could finance
a small army or purchase a small province. It is no surprise that the gates
of heaven were thought to be made of pearl.

With the discovery of the New World, another major source of pearls
became available for exploitation. It is not coincidence that the name
Margarita was given to a Venezuelan island. The name Margaret is
derived from the Greek word for pearl. (Indeed, the name "margarine" is
derived from the same source. Early producers, faced with a butter
substitute which was disconcertingly white, thought that describing its
hue as "pearly" would be a good marketing ploy.) Isla Margarita, or Pearl

Island, lies at the heart of an area from which the Spanish extracted thousands of New World pearls during the sixteenth century. For a while, the value of pearls being shipped back to Spain from the Americas exceeded even that of silver and gold.

Colombia and Panama also proved good sources for pearls, while Mexico became famous for black pearls from the Sea of Cortez. But it was not only the Spanish possessions that yielded pearls. In North America, fine freshwater pearls were discovered in considerable quantities. Small "pearl rushes" followed the initial finds, and while thousands of pearls were added to the market, whole species of mussels were wiped out in the search for riches. Still, it is American mussel species that play a major, almost universal role in the modern pearl industry.

As well as producing round pearls, American mussels were champion makers of mother-of-pearl shell. Before the invention of plastics, this material was prized for the manufacture of buttons, and a large industry was based on the harvesting of Mississippi mussels. In its heyday, the small Iowa city of Muscatine had the remarkable distinction of producing more than a third of the entire world's supply of fine buttons. Even today, the freshwater pearl is the official gemstone of the state of Tennessee, where efforts have been made to bring the pearl farming industry back to the United States.

By the eighteenth century, overfishing and pollution had depleted the New World of its natural pearl resources. The following century saw the development of new sources in the South Pacific and Australia, but real increase in the production of pearls would have to depend on innovation rather than exploration (see "The Making of a Gem," page 108).

FOR A WHILE, THE VALUE OF PEARLS BEING SHIPPED BACK TO SPAIN EXCEEDED EVEN THAT OF SILVER AND GOLD.

DESIGNING WITH

PEARLS

MIXING PEARLS
WITH OTHER BEADS

A bead is deceptively simple. It is just a small object with a hole through it. Yet for more than 40,000 years, human beings have been fascinated and sometimes obsessed with them. Simple they may be, but beads have always been the most popular and prominent element of jewelry design.

Pearls could make a good claim to be the mother of all beads. Most are drilled as beads, and they are certainly one of the very oldest materials to be used this way. Indeed, in some parts of the world, the word "pearl" is synonymous with "bead." The recently coined name for an academic who studies beads is margaretologist, derived, as are the names Margaret and margarine, from the Greek word for "pearl." Although pearls are the king and queen of beads, there are, of course, many other types to consider.

Indeed, the range of materials used to make beads is overwhelming: stones, metals, seeds, shells, teeth, tusks, clay, plastics, snake vertebrae, wood, and glass—the list even includes a bizarre substance exuded from the body of an Indian beetle. Add to this variety the artistry of countless designers and the lexicon of beads becomes truly staggering. There are literally billions of styles in limitless combinations of colors, shapes, textures, patterns, densities, and luminosities.

But not all of them should share the stage with the pearl. The designs in this chapter introduce you to some of the materials, shapes, and colors of beads that enhance the look of pearl jewelry. The ingredients list for each design provides enough description for you to be able to find not just the pearls but all of the complementary beads, whether at your local bead store or from a mail order/Internet supplier. If you have trouble finding an exact match, do not be afraid of substituting similar beads of equal quality.

Since pearls are considered gems, it is natural to find them in combination with precious metals and with other gemstones. The choice of stone is based upon quality and color. Try and select gemstones that will complement and enhance the color values of your pearls. If a pearl has rose overtones, then pink tourmaline will enhance that color. A pearl with a lot of orient, that rainbow-like iridescence, will be enhanced by materials in the green/yellow part of the spectrum, such as green garnet and gold. If you prefer to emphasize the blue tones in a pearl, iolite or sapphires will bring that out. Rubies play up pearls with tones from the redder, warmer parts of the rainbow.

Size is a primary consideration. You do not want the other gemstones to overwhelm the pearls, so there needs to be a balance between them. Sometimes this balance is struck by using large pearls and several smaller gemstones, sometimes with large gemstones and many smaller pearls. It is not only the relationship between individual pearls and gemstones that counts, but the overall effect of the design.

Shape is also important. Although there is a place in pearl designs for plain rounds, I usually prefer to work with facetted gemstones simply because their reflectivity stands a better chance of matching up to the luster of the pearls.

A high-quality glass crystal bead can also make a fine companion for less expensive and faux pearls. These come in a large range of colors, and the bicone shape seems to work particularly well. Not only do the cut crystal surfaces offer a lot of sparkle, but they can even add iridescence if you use those with an AB (for "aurora borealis") coating.

The important thing to remember about pearls is that they should be treated with respect. While their look can be lighthearted and shamelessly romantic, they are seldom playful and never cheap. The materials described here offer a certain level of dignity that will lend your designs the elegance expected of pearl jewelry.

WHEN MAKING SUBSTITUTIONS OR STARTING YOUR OWN DESIGNS, CONSIDER THESE PROVEN COMBINATIONS:

COMBINE WITH REAL PEARLS OF HIGH VALUE
Gold
Sterling silver
High-value gemstones

COMBINE WITH REAL PEARLS OF MEDIUM VALUE
Gold-filled and vermeil beads
Sterling silver
Medium-value gemstones

COMBINE WITH FAUX PEARLS AND SMALL, INEXPENSIVE REAL PEARLS
Vermeil
Sterling Silver
Glass crystal (such as Swarovski)

14.
PEARLS WITH GREEN GARNETS

THIS SIMPLY SENSATIONAL NECKLACE MAKES A STATEMENT. CLUSTERED IN THREES BETWEEN LARGE-DIAMETER COIN PEARLS, GREEN GARNET BRIOLETTES CREATE A BROAD BAND OF GEMS AROUND THE NECK. IF YOU ARE NOT IN THE AUTUMN/WINTER MOOD THAT GREEN GARNETS CREATES, SUBSTITUTE OTHER GEMSTONES SUCH AS PINK TOURMALINE OR APATITE.

1. Attach one half of the clasp top the beading wire with a crimp bead. String on a gold spacer bead, a coin pearl, another gold spacer, and three briolettes. Repeat this pattern thirteen times and end with a gold spacer, coin pearl, and gold spacer.

2. Before attaching the other half of the clasp, lay your necklace out and make sure that the trios of briolettes are arranged so that the outer two lie one side of the strand, with the middle one on the opposite side (as shown in the photograph). When everything is arranged properly, tighten the beading wire so there are no gaps between any of the beads, and use a crimp bead to attach it to the other half of the toggle clasp. Slip the crimp covers over the crimps, and gently close them shut with your pliers.

TOOLS
Wire Cutters, Crimping Pliers

MATERIALS

15	10mm coin pearls (less than half a 16" strand)
42	6–9mm green garnet briolettes (about a 9" strand)
30	vermeil Thai spacer beads (3–5mm side-drilled cylinders)
2	gold-filled crimp beads
2	gold-filled crimp bead covers
1	gold-filled toggle clasp
20"	beading wire

NOTE
Green garnet is also known as grossular garnet.

THE COLOR OF GEMSTONES

DIFFERENT GEMSTONES WILL ENHANCE DIFFERENT COLOR TONES OF YOUR PEARLS. ONCE YOU HAVE DECIDED ON THE PARTICULAR COLOR WITHIN THE PEARL YOU WISH TO EMPHASIZE, USE THE CHART BELOW TO FIND A STONE THAT WILL COMPLEMENT IT. AS WITH PEARLS, THE AVAILABILITY OF GEMSTONES AND THE VARIETY OF COLORS HAS INCREASED GREATLY IN THE LAST FEW YEARS THANKS TO MODERN PRODUCTION TECHNIQUES.

(listed by primary color tones)

REDS AND PINKS
Ruby
Garnet
Rhodochrosite
Coral
Rose Quartz
Pink Sapphire
Pink Tourmaline
Morganite
Spinel

BLUES AND PURPLES
Iolite
Sapphire
Blue Topaz
Kyanite
Lapis Lazuli
Turquoise
Aquamarine
Amethyst
Tanzanite
Blue Topaz
Indicolite

GREENS
Green Garnet
Peridot
Emerald
Chrome Diopside

YELLOWS, ORANGES, AND BROWNS
Citrine
Brandy Quartz
Smoky Quartz
Amber
Hessonite
Carnelian

CLEARS/WHITES/NEUTRALS
Diamond
Clear Zircon
Clear Topaz
Rainbow Moonstone
Milky Quartz

IRIDESCENTS
Opal
Labradorite

15.
PEARL STRAND WITH GEM CLUSTER

THE BEAUTIFUL READYMADE CENTERPIECE IN THIS DESIGN FEATURES TINY PEARLS CLUSTERED AROUND A LITTLE DIAMOND SET IN EIGHTEEN-KARAT GOLD. A PRETTY STRAND OF SMALL, INEXPENSIVE PEARLS CAN BE USED AS A WONDERFUL FRAME FOR SUCH A CENTERPIECE.

1. Attach the beading wire to the clasp using a gold bead and crimp.

2. Add a gold daisy spacer, ruby rondel, and gold spacer. Now add about 7¹⁄₂ inches of pearls. Add a spacer/ruby/spacer combination. Then add 3 pearls, a gold bead, and the centerpiece.

3. String on the other half of the necklace to exactly mirror the first. Attach the other half of the clasp.

CENTERPIECES

CENTERPIECE NECKLACES FOCUS THE EYE WHEREVER THEIR CENTER FALLS. THE DESIGNS ON THESE AND THE NEXT TWO PAGES ATTRACT THE GAZE MODESTLY TO THE NECK, BUT CENTERPIECE NECKLACES CAN BE AS DARING AS YOU WISH. IF YOUR DRESS OR MOOD CALLS FOR A LONGER STYLE, JUST ADD MORE INGREDIENTS.

TOOLS
Wire Cutters, Crimping Pliers

MATERIALS

1	16" strand of 2 or 3mm white freshwater near-round or rondel pearls
4	3mm facetted ruby rondels
8	2.5mm 18K gold or vermeil daisy spacer beads
4	2mm gold round beads
1	diamond-and-pearl cluster centerpiece
1	16mm gold hook-and-eye clasp
2	gold-filled bead crimps
20"	beading wire

NOTE
Readymade centerpieces are widely available. Many, like this lovely piece from Jaipur, are produced by traditional Indian artisans whose skills have been handed down through the generations.

16.
GEMSTONES WITH PEARL CENTERPIECE

A SINGLE, MEDIUM-SIZE PEARL LOOKS GORGEOUS WITH THIS GRADUATED STRAND OF MACHINE-CUT, FACETED TANZANITE RONDELS. GEMSTONES IN BLUES AND REDS COMPLEMENT THE IRIDESCENCE OF PEARLS VERY NICELY, WHILE GREENS, YELLOWS, AND CRYSTALS DO NOT.

1. Divide the graduated gemstone strand into two exactly even halves. The easiest way to do this is to tie a piece of thread around the strand beside the center bead. Alternatively, you can take them all off the strand and lay them out on a bead board. If you need to, remove one large bead from the center to make the two halves even. (You can use this bead later in another design.)

2. Attach one end of the beading wire to the clasp using one of the gold beads to cover the end of the wire (see page 116). Add one half of the strand of graduated beads, starting with the smaller beads first (so that they lie closest to the clasp). Now add a gold round bead and a bead cap. Add the pearl so that it fits snugly against the concave side of the bead cap. Add the other bead cap, concave side against the pearl. Then add a gold round bead, followed by the other half of the graduated gemstone strand, with the smallest beads going on last.

3. Finish off the necklace by adding the gold bead and bead crimp. Attach the other half of the hook-and-eye clasp by looping the wire through the ring and back through the crimp and the gold bead. Make sure everything is tight. Pull the end of the beading wire taut with a pair of pliers, squeeze shut the crimp, and snip off the wire as close to the gold bead as possible.

TOOLS
Wire Cutters, Crimping Pliers

MATERIALS

1	16" strand of graduated gemstone beads Note: this design uses faceted tanzanite rondels (machine cut for better quality) ranging in size from 3.5–5mm
1	good-quality round pearl, 7 to 8mm in size (pictured is a 7mm Akoya)
4	2.5mm gold-filled round beads
2	4.5mm gold-filled bead caps
2	gold-filled bead crimps
1	gold-filled hook-and-eye clasp
20"	.013 beading wire

TIP
Pearls can be either the frame for the centerpiece or the centerpiece itself. Large pearls beg to be at center stage, but in a good design, you can also effectively use a cluster of little pearls or even a single medium-size pearl. Be sure to use a high-quality pearl large enough to stand out from the surrounding gemstones, the quality of which should match, but not exceed, that of the pearl.

17.
PRIMA BALLERINA NECKLACE

THE STYLE OF THIS NECKLACE DEPENDS UPON FINDING A DISTINCTIVE PEARL TO ACT AS PRIMA BALLERINA. THE 12 BY 9 MILLIMETER PEARL DROP AT THE CENTER OF THIS DESIGN IS A FRESHWATER BEAUTY WITH A LOVELY LUSTER AND ORIENT THAT EASILY OUTSHINES ALL THE OTHER PEARLS. I GAVE THIS ONE A SPECIAL "HEADDRESS"—A GOLD BEAD CAP STUDDED WITH TINY DIAMONDS.

1. To make the centerpiece, add the large pearl to the headpin. Next, add the bead cap and a gold bead. Finish it off by making a very small wire-wrapped loop (pages 126–127). The reason you make a wrapped loop is for security—you certainly don't want this kind of pearl to fall off your necklace.

2. Attach the wire to the clasp with a bead crimp. String about 7 1/2 inches of teardrop pearls, then a gold bead and the pearl centerpiece.

3. Add another gold bead and another 7 1/2 inches of teardrop pearls. Hold the necklace around your neck to judge its length and symmetry, and finish it off by attaching it to the other half of the clasp with the remaining bead crimp.

TOOLS

Wire Cutters, Round-Nose Pliers, Flat-Nosed Pliers, Crimping Pliers

MATERIALS

- 1   12 by 9mm freshwater pearl drop (or another pearl of distinctive size and quality)
- 1   16" strand of 4mm top-drilled freshwater teardrop pearls
- 1   gold 9mm bead cap
- 3   2mm gold round beads
- 1   15mm gold hook-and-eye clasp
- 1   gold 1" head pin with ball tip
- 2   gold-filled bead crimps
- 20" beading wire

18.
PEARL AND TOURMALINE NECKLACE

PEARLS CAN PROVIDE GREAT SUPPORT FOR A LARGE AND IMPRESSIVE GEMSTONE. HERE I USED A SHARD-LIKE PIECE OF TOURMALINE WITH ASYMMETRICAL FACETS AS A CENTERPIECE.

1. Cut the beading wire into three 20-inch pieces. Divide your tourmaline strand into three roughly equal parts. Divide the pearls into three roughly equal parts by cutting the strands into thirds. Start the first strand by using three gold beads and a crimp to attach a piece of the wire to the top loop of the clasp. Use one third of the tourmaline beads, one third of the pearls, and about eight of the gold beads. String them on the wire to create a pleasing random pattern. You can use the photograph for guidance, or rely on your own judgment. (The colors of your tourmaline strand will certainly be somewhat different than the one I have used.) Try the strand around your neck and add or subtract beads as necessary. When you are happy with the length, add the three gold beads and the crimp, and attach to the top loop of the other half of the clasp.

2. Make another strand in the same way, attaching it to the middle loop of the clasp. Try it around your neck to make sure it is falls parallel to the first strand.

3. The third strand is made the same way as the first two, with the following exception. When you reach the middle of the strand, add the gemstone centerpiece with a gold bead on either side. Attach this strand to the bottom loops of the clasp. The middle of the strand should be 7 1/2 inches from the beginning gold bead, but check the length around your neck to make sure that the centerpiece lies at the center of the necklace.

TOOLS
Wire Cutters, Crimping Pliers

MATERIALS

1	large piece of top-drilled, facetted tourmaline (or other gemstone)
2	16" strands of 2.5mm round freshwater pearls
1	16" multicolor strand of 3mm faceted tourmaline rondels
56	2mm gold round beads
1	20mm gold-filled 3-row sliding clasp
6	gold bead crimps
60"	beading wire

NOTE
When you wear this necklace, the weight of the centerpiece will pull the third strand down to fall slightly below the other two strands, emphasizing its status.

19.
PEARL AND MARCASITE RONDEL BRACELET

UNLIKE A TWO-STRAND NECKLACE, THE STRANDS OF THIS SEVEN-INCH BRACELET NEED TO BE ROUGHLY THE SAME LENGTH TO FORM PARALLEL ROWS AROUND YOUR WRIST.

1. Cut the beading wire into two 10-inch lengths, and use the crimp to attach one piece to the top loop of the clasp. String on a pearl and a rondel. Repeat this until you have strung 29 pearls. Make sure the pearls and rondels all fit snugly together. Try the bracelet around your wrist. If it is the right size, add the crimp and attach the strand to the other half of the clasp, taking care to attach it to the appropriate loop.

2. Make a second strand in the same way as the first and attach it to the remaining loops of the clasp.

USING SPACERS

IN THESE DESIGNS, I'VE USED SPACER BEADS AS KEY ELEMENTS OF THE OVERALL DESIGN. THEY CAN EITHER PLAY A VERY PROMINENT AND OBVIOUS ROLE, AS IN THE BRACELET WITH MARCASITE RONDELS, OR A SUBTLE, ALMOST UNSEEN ROLE, AS IN THE THREE-STRAND NECKLACE. EITHER WAY, SPACER BEADS ARE A VITAL PART OF THE JEWELRY DESIGNER'S PALETTE.

TOOLS
Wire Cutters, Crimping Pliers

MATERIALS
42   7.5mm silver-gray freshwater pearls with a light purple hue (about 3/4 of a 16" strand)

40   6mm Thai silver-and-marcasite rondels

4   silver crimp beads

4   sterling silver crimp bead covers

1   sterling silver 2-loop sliding clasp

20"   beading wire

NOTE
Because of the variation in pearl sizes, one strand of the bracelet will probably end up being a little longer than the other. Your wrist is not a perfect cylinder, so if you wear the bracelet the right way around, this difference in length will fit into the wrist's natural contours.

20.
CRYSTAL AND PEARL NECKLACE

THE TINY SILVER-PLATED CHARLOTTES IN THIS THREE-STRAND
NECKLACE ARE JUST A LITTLE OVER A MILLIMETER IN SIZE, BUT
THEY SERVE AN IMPORTANT PURPOSE: THEY FRAME EACH OF THE
SWAROVSKI CRYSTAL BEADS, EMPHASIZING THEIR BICONE
SHAPE AND GIVING THEM SPACE TO CREATE AN IMPRESSION.

1. Cut the beading wire into two pieces, one measuring 20 inches
    and the other 44 inches. Divide the crystals into three groups of
    26, 28, and 30 beads, respectively. Use the crimp to attach the
    shorter length of beading wire to the clasp loop. String 3 silver
    charlotte spacers, then alternate pearls with the set of 26
    crystals to fill the rest of the strand to about 15 ¹/₂ inches.
    **Remember to put a silver spacer bead on either side of each
    crystal!** If you're not confident about creating a random pattern
    right on the wire, arrange the beads in a row first until you are
    happy with the grouping. Try the strand around your neck to test
    its size. Check to make sure each crystal has one spacer bead on
    each side. If you finish the necklace and then find you missed
    even one sequence of spacer, crystal, spacer, it will ruin your
    day! Finish by adding 3 more spacer beads and a crimp and
    attaching the strand to the other side of the clasp.

2. Take the long strand of beading wire and fold it in half. Pass the
    folded "V"-shape end of the wire through a crimp and attach to
    the top loop of one side of the clasp. Using the instructions
    above, string a strand of pearls and crystals with the group of 28
    crystals. Make this strand 1 inch longer than the first strand. As
    you add your beads, lay them alongside the first strand to make
    sure that the random patterns are harmonious. Check for length
    (and to make sure that all the crystals have spacers on either
    side), and attach the strand to the other half of the clasp.

3. Make the final strand 1 inch longer than the second strand,
    using the remaining pearls, spacers, and the final 30 crystals.
    Check the size and the spacers; attach the strand to the clasp.

TOOLS
Wire Cutters, Crimping Pliers

MATERIALS

2	16" strands of 2–3mm rondel white freshwater pearls
84	4mm tanzanite Swarovski crystal bicone beads
196	silver-plated charlottes (14/0)
6	sterling silver crimp beads
1	10mm sterling silver toggle clasp
64"	beading wire

NOTE
The three strands of this necklace, although
different lengths, are attached to the loops of a
single row clasp so that they stand out as three
separate rows when worn.

21.
PEARLS WITH CHARLOTTES

CHARLOTTES CREATE WIDE INTERVALS BETWEEN THE PEARLS
AND GEMSTONES IN THIS DESIGN. THE CHARLOTTES ALSO CREATE
A THIN GOLD "CHAIN"—WHICH MAKES AN ECONOMY OF PEARLS
GO A LONG WAY. THE ADDED TOUCH OF GOLD DAISY SPACERS
HIGHLIGHTS THE PEARLS AND GEMSTONES.

1. Use a gold round bead and a crimp to attach the beading wire to
   the clasp. Add ingredients in the following order:
   - Garnet, 1 inch of charlottes, d, p, d, $^1/_2$ inch charlottes
   - Tourmaline, d, tourmaline, 1 inch charlottes
   - Garnet, d, p, d, garnet, $^1/_2$ inch charlottes, garnet, $^1/_2$ inch
     charlottes
   - Tourmaline, d, tourmaline, $^1/_2$ inch charlottes, garnet, $^1/_2$ inch
     charlottes
   - Garnet, $^1/_2$ inch charlottes, garnet, d, p, d, garnet, $^1/_2$ inch
     charlottes, tourmaline, d, tourmaline, $^1/_2$ inch charlottes,
     garnet, d, p, d, garnet, d, p, d, garnet, d, p, d, garnet

   Now that you have added onto the central part of your necklace,
   try it around your neck to see if it falls in the right place. Check
   that the pattern is correct.

2. Complete the other side of your necklace as follows:
   - $^1/_2$ inch charlottes, tourmaline, d, tourmaline,
     $^1/_2$ inch charlottes
   - Garnet, d, p, d, garnet, $^1/_2$ inch charlottes, garnet
   - $^1/_2$ inch charlottes, tourmaline, d, tourmaline,
     $^1/_2$ inch charlottes
   - Garnet, d, p, d, garnet, 1 inch charlottes, tourmaline,
     d, tourmaline
   - $^1/_2$ inch charlottes, d, p, d, 1 inch charlottes, garnet
   - Gold round bead and crimp

   Whew! Double-check the strand for size. Make sure that the
   pattern is correct and symmetrical, then attach to the other part
   of the clasp.

TOOLS
Wire Cutters, Crimping Pliers

MATERIALS

9	6mm round or potato-shaped freshwater pearls with a natural rose hue (abbreviated in recipe as "p")
11"	gold-plated charlotte beads (13/0)
17	4mm faceted round garnet beads
12	4mm faceted rondel pink tourmaline beads
24	4mm vermeil daisy spacer beads (abbreviated in recipe as "d")
2	gold-filled 3mm round beads
2	gold-filled crimp beads
1	6mm gold-filled spring ring clasp
20"	.015 49-strand beading wire

22.
PEARLS
AND DAISIES

I LOVE USING DAISY BEADS IN GROUPS. HERE THEY FORM A
THICK GOLD ROPE STUDDED WITH LOVELY NATURAL PURPLE
HUES, A COLOR SOMETIMES CALLED LAVENDER.

1. Use a 3-millimeter gold round bead and a crimp to attach the
    beading wire to the clasp. Next, add a 4-millimeter gold round
    bead. String the daisies and pearls as follows:
    - 13d, p, 5d, p
    - 3d, p, 5d, p
    - Repeat this pattern a total of 6 times. End with 5d. Since the
      last pearl will be at the center of your necklace, stop for a
      moment and try it around your neck to see that it falls in the
      right place. Double-check the pattern.

2. Complete the other side of the necklace as follows: 3d, p, 5d, p.
    Repeat this pattern for a total of 6 repeats. End with 13d. Check
    for length, and then add a 4-millimeter gold round, a
    3-millimeter gold round, and a bead crimp. Attach to the other
    half of the clasp.

TOOLS
Wire Cutters, Crimping Pliers

MATERIALS

31	7.5mm near-round or potato-shaped freshwater pearls with a natural purple hue (abbreviated in recipe as "p")
148	4mm vermeil daisy spacer beads (abbreviated in recipe as "d")
2	4mm and 2–3mm gold-filled round beads
2	gold-filled crimp beads
2	gold-filled crimp bead covers
1	12mm vermeil toggle clasp
20"	beading wire

23.
STICK PEARLS
AND "CORNFLAKES"

THIS DESIGN USES TWO FLAT PEARL SHAPES, STICKS, AND A TYPE
OF KESHI KNOWN AS "CORNFLAKES," IN AN IRIDESCENT
CHAMPAGNE COLOR COMPLEMENTED BY BLUE ZIRCON BEADS.
THE DANGLING BEADS ARE ATTACHED LIKE A CENTERPIECE.

1. First, refer to "Wire Wrapping" on page 127. Start the centerpiece
    by making the outside "tassels" as follows. Attach a cornflake
    pearl to the wire by making a wrapped loop and another loop.
    Link 1 zircon bead, 1 cornflake pearl, 1 zircon bead, 1 cornflake
    pearl, and then 1 zircon. Link this last zircon bead to the outside
    ring of the bail. Make an identical tassel, and link it to the other
    outside loop of the bail. To make the center tassel, start with a
    zircon drop and link it to a stick pearl. Link that pearl to another
    stick pearl. Link that to a zircon bead, and then link the zircon
    bead to the center loop of the bail. Put the centerpiece aside.

2. To start the necklace, thread the beading wire through a bead
    crimp, then through 10 of the very small seed beads. Pass the wire
    through the ring of the hook part of the clasp. Bring the end of the
    beading wire back through the crimp bead, the gold spacer, and
    the crystal bead. Make sure everything is tight and there are no
    spaces between the beads. The seed beads should neatly cover
    the beading wire as it passes though the clasp ring. Squeeze your
    crimp bead until it secures the beading wire to the clasp.

3. Add 1 gold spacer bead and 1 crystal bead to hide the tail of the
    beading wire. Snip off any excess tail after the crystal bead. Add
    1 zircon rondel, 2 seed beads, 1 stick pearl, 2 seed beads, 1
    rondel, and 2 seed beads. Repeat until you have 5 stick pearls.
    Add 2 cornflake pearls. Add another stick pearl pattern, then 3
    cornflake pearls followed by 1 seed bead, 1 rondel and 5–6 seed
    beads. Now add the centerpiece. The top ring of the bail should
    be big enough for the seed beads to pass through. If it isn't, take
    off 3 seed beads and put the centerpiece ring directly onto the
    beading wire, adding the 3 seed beads back after. Repeat the
    pattern for the other side of the necklace. To finish, attach the
    end of the beading wire to the "eye" of the clasp.

TOOLS

Wire Cutters, Round-Nose Pliers,
Flat-Nosed Pliers

MATERIALS

14 stick pearls approximately 20mm in
    length (about three-quarters of a
    16" strand)

16 cornflake pearls

36 dark iridescent charlotte seed beads
    (or any very small seed beads that
    complement the pearls and gemstones)

25 4mm faceted rondel natural blue zircon
    beads

2   4mm erinite AB Swarovski crystal beads

1   faceted zircon drop (approximately
    9–12mm)

1   gold-filled hook-and-eye clasp

2   gold 3mm faceted spacer beads

2   ft of beading wire

2   ft of 26-gauge gold wire

1   triple-loop gold bail

2   gold-filled bead crimps

1   gold hook-and-eye clasp

24.
STICK PEARLS
WITH BALI BEADS

SILVER BEADS MADE BY THE GRANULATION PROCESS ARE
SOMETIMES REFERRED TO AS "BALI" BEADS (ALTHOUGH MANY
BALI BEADS ARE PRODUCED ELSEWHERE). TO CREATE THIS
INTRICATE PATTERN, TINY, ROUND GRANULES OF SILVER ARE
FUSED TO THE BODY OF THE BEAD.

1. Cut the wire into twenty 2-inch pieces and one 4-inch piece.
   Using 15 of the 2-inch pieces of wire, all the round pearls, and 1
   stick pearl, make 15 wire-wrapped links in the following pattern:
   loop, round bead, daisy spacer, pearl, daisy spacer, round bead,
   and loop. Snip away any excess wire.

2. Using 4 of the 2-inch pieces of wire and all the Bali-style silver
   beads, make 4 wire-wrapped links of the following pattern:
   loop, round bead, Bali bead, round bead, and loop. Snip away
   any excess wire.

3. Using the 4-inch piece of wire and 3 stick pearls, make a wire-
   wrapped link of the following pattern: loop, round bead, daisy
   spacer, pearl, daisy spacer, pearl, daisy spacer, pearl, daisy
   spacer, round bead, and loop. Snip away any excess wire.

4. To the eyepin, add 1 round pearl, 1 daisy spacer, and 1 round
   bead, then make a wrapped loop. Using the headpins, make 3
   tiny dangles by adding a 2-millimeter silver bead and making a
   wrapped loop. Open the eye of the eyepin and add the dangles.

5. To assemble the necklace, use the 5-millimeter split rings to
   attach the links as follows: clasp connector, round pearl, Bali
   bead, 5 round pearls, Bali bead, 5 round pearls, "Bali" bead,
   round pearl, stick pearl, 2 round pearls, and clasp connector.

6. Assemble the centerpiece by using 5-millimeter split rings to
   attach the pearl with the dangles to the remaining Bali bead
   and then to the triple stick pearl link. Next, add the 7-millimeter
   split ring. To attach the centerpiece, open the spring ring clasp
   and hook it to the 7-millimeter split ring.

TOOLS

Wire Cutters, Round-Nosed Pliers, Flat-Nosed
Pliers

MATERIALS

15	9–10mm white potato-shaped pearls
4	white stick pearls about 22–29mm in length
4	9mm Bali-style silver beads
6	5mm silver "dangle" beads
41	3mm silver round beads
35	5mm silver daisy spacer beads
3	2mm silver round beads
21	5mm and one 7mm sterling silver split rings
42"	26-gauge sterling silver wire
1	1" sterling silver eyepin with decorated eye
3	$^1/_2$" sterling silver eyepin with decoration and eye that opens
1	16mm sterling silver spring ring clasp

25.
FACETED PEARLS
ON WIRE

WHEN YOU USE EITHER GOLD-FILLED OR STERLING SILVER WIRE,
IT BECOMES AN INTEGRAL PART OF THE DESIGN. IN THIS DESIGN,
THE LUSTER OF THE FACETED PEARLS HAS GEM-LIKE
REFLECTIONS. (ALL FACETED PEARLS ARE FRESHWATER SINCE
THEY NEED TO HAVE VERY THICK NACRE.) THE COLORS OF THE
LITTLE DANGLES OF GEMSTONE BRIOLETTES ARE ARRANGED
ASYMMETRICALLY, WHICH GIVES THE NECKLACE A DYNAMIC LOOK.
FEEL FREE TO SELECT COLORS THAT SUIT YOUR TASTE.

1. Start by making the pearl links. Use 1 ½ inches of gold-filled
    wire for each pearl and create a 3- to 3.5-millimeter loop on
    either side (see "Wire-Wrapping," page 127.) Cut only a couple
    of pieces of wire at the beginning to test the optimum length for
    your pearls.

2. When you have finished the links, use the headpins to make the
    tiny dangles. Put on 1 gemstone briolette and 1 gold bead, then
    make a 2- to 2.5-millimeter loop and wrap the remaining wire
    around the base of the loop.

3. Start making the necklace by taking 1 of the wrapped pearls and
    adding an open jump ring to one end. Slip another wrapped
    pearl onto the jump ring and close it. Repeat this process 2 more
    times.

4. After adding the open jump ring to the fourth pearl, slip on 1 of
    the gemstone dangles. Add the next pearl and close the jump
    ring (see illustration). Repeat this pattern 17 times. Now add 4
    more pearls and jump rings without any dangles. Add a final
    open jump ring. Slip on the last of your gemstone dangles, then
    the spring ring clasp, and close the jump ring. When you wear
    your necklace, the clasp will attach to the loop at the end of the
    first wire-wrapped pearl.

TOOLS
Wire Cutters, Round-Nosed Pliers,
Flat-Nosed Pliers

MATERIALS

25	5.5mm faceted freshwater pearls (about a third of a 16" multicolor strand)
19	4–5mm multicolor tourmaline briolettes
25	3.5mm gold-filled jump rings
19	½" gold-filled headpins
19	2.5mm gold-filled round beads
1	6mm gold-filled spring ring clasp
40"	gold-filled 24-gauge wire

26.
A LOT OF WORK—
BUT WORTH IT!

THIS NECKLACE REALLY DOES TAKE A LONG TIME TO MAKE, BUT IT
ALSO ATTRACTS A LOT OF ENTHUSIASTIC ADMIRATION WHEN
WORN. ALTHOUGH NEITHER THE PEARLS NOR THE LITTLE
GEMSTONES ARE COSTLY, THE ALL-NATURAL COLORS AND
ELABORATE CONSTRUCTION OF THIS DESIGN MAKE IT LOOK LIKE A
VERY EXPENSIVE PIECE OF JEWELRY.

1. Start by making the little pendants, using the same method for
   each. Take a headpin and add a mixture of baroque pearls,
   gemstones, and gold beads and spacers. (Use the photograph on
   page 79 as inspiration for appealing mixtures.) Then make a
   wire-wrapped loop about 2 to 3 millimeters in diameter. The
   secret to this design is that the length of the pendants varies
   from $3/8$ to $7/8$ of an inch. This prevents them from clashing when
   they are on the necklace. I suggest you make equal numbers of
   the pendants in 3 lengths—long, medium, and short. Or you
   can line the dangles up as you make them to see how they will
   fit together.

2. Using the crimp backed by a 3-millimeter gold bead, attach the
   beading wire to the clasp. Add 1 daisy spacer, 1 round pearl, and
   1 pendant. Repeat the round-pearl-and-pendant pattern until
   you have used up all your pendants. Hold the necklace up
   frequently to make sure that the arrangement of the pendants is
   working well. Check the length of the necklace around your
   neck. Finish off with 1 pearl, 1 spacer, and 1 round gold bead,
   and attach the end to the other half of the clasp with a crimp.
   Add the crimp covers. Go out to dinner to show off the result of
   all your work!

TOOLS

Wire Cutters, Crimping Pliers , Round-Nosed
Pliers, Flat-Nosed Pliers

MATERIALS

1	16" strand of 5.5mm near-round natural pink-color freshwater pearls
1	16" strand of 5–7mm mixed natural and dyed color baroque pearls
1	mixture of "leftover" small gemstones and pearls (garnet, rainbow moonstone, iolite)
40	4mm vermeil daisy spacer beads
12	assorted other 4mm vermeil spacers and bead caps
12	2mm gold-filled round beads
67	1" gold-filled head pins
2	gold-filled crimp beads
2	3mm gold-filled round beads
2	gold-filled crimp bead covers
1	15mm vermeil toggle clasp
20"	beading wire

27.
PEARLS ON LEATHER CORD

THE HOLES IN PEARLS ARE ALWAYS PRETTY SMALL: SINCE PEARL
PRODUCERS OFTEN SELL THE GEMS BY WEIGHT, IT WOULD BE
SELF-DEFEATING TO DRILL OUT AN EXCESSIVE AMOUNT OF THE
PROFIT! CORDS ARE TOO THICK TO THREAD THROUGH PEARLS,
BUT THEY CAN BE USED EFFECTIVELY TO DISPLAY THEM.

1. First make the 13 pearl drops (see "Using Headpins and
   Eyepins," page 126). Add 1 silver daisy to a headpin, followed by
   1 pearl. Make a small loop. Repeat until you have 13 drops.
   When you have finished all the drops, hook them onto the silver
   cord tube by opening and closing the loops.

2. Attach half the clasp to the end of the leather cord by squeezing
   the crimp part with flat-nosed pliers. Slide on the silver tube. Try
   it around your neck for size and finish off by attaching the other
   half of the clasp.

TOOLS
Round-Nosed Pliers, Flat-Nosed Pliers

MATERIALS

13	6mm white near-round freshwater pearls
13	4mm sterling silver daisy spacer beads
13	$1/2$" sterling silver headpins with ball tips
1	sterling silver cord tube with 13 loops
1	sterling silver leather crimp clasp
16"	1.5mm leather cord (European quality)

28.
PEARLS ON SNAKE CHAIN

THE GOLD CORD ALSO KNOWN AS SNAKE CHAIN COMES
WITH THE CLASP ALREADY ATTACHED. ONE SIDE OF THE CLASP
UNSCREWS TO LET YOU STRING THE BEADS ONTO THE CORD.
MAKING THIS NECKLACE REQUIRES PATIENCE—IT HAS 75 WIRE-
WRAPPED LOOPS—BUT IT WILL IMPROVE YOUR LOOPING SKILLS!

1. First make all the little dangles by attaching a bead or beads to
    a headpin and making a small loop (see page 126). Use your
    own judgment to create a variety of different types of dangles: a
    single pearl; a single crystal; a single gold bead; 1 pearl and 1
    gold bead; 1 crystal bead and 1 gold bead. (See the photo on
    page 82 for guidance.) The loops should have a short wrap. As
    you make them, be sure that the loops are big enough to slide
    on to the gold cord.

2. Unscrew the clasp. Add 1 gold tube bead, and then arrange all
    the dangles in a pleasing manner. Add the other gold tube bead,
    and screw the clasp back on.

TOOLS
Round-Nosed Pliers

MATERIALS

42	3mm freshwater pearls with natural purple hue
32	3mm light amethyst Swarovski crystal bicone beads
32	gold-filled 2.5mm round beads
77	gold headpins with ball tip
2	7 by 5mm gold tube beads
1	16" gold snake chain with unscrewing hook-and-eye clasp attached

MOTHER-OF-PEARL EARRINGS | FAUX PEARL AND CHAIN EARRINGS | TAHITIAN PEARL EARRINGS

POTATO PEARL AND CHAIN EARRINGS | ROUND PEARL AND CHAIN EARRINGS | COIN PEARL AND CHAIN EARRINGS

EYEPINS

AN EYEPIN IS JUST A HEADPIN WITH A LOOP AT THE BOTTOM INSTEAD OF A FLATTENED TIP. IF YOU DO NOT HAVE AN EYEPIN AVAILABLE, SIMPLY TAKE A HEADPIN, CUT OFF THE FLATTENED TIP, AND USE YOUR ROUND-NOSED PLIERS TO MAKE A SMALL LOOP. IT WILL BE SLIGHTLY SHORTER THAN THE HEADPIN BUT SHOULD WORK NICELY. IF YOU DON'T HAVE A HEADPIN, TRY MAKING YOUR EYEPINS USING THE SAME METHOD ON A SIMPLE PIECE OF WIRE. JUST CUT A COUPLE OF 2-INCH SEGMENTS, AND FORM SMALL LOOPS AT ONE END.

29.
MOTHER-OF-PEARL EARRINGS

THIS RICH, IRIDESCENT MOTHER-OF-PEARL COMES FROM THE INSIDE OF ABALONE SHELLS. THESE LARGE COMPOSITE BEADS ARE CREATED BY CUTTING THE MOTHER-OF-PEARL NACRE INTO SMALL PIECES TO FORM A MOSAIC. THUS, YOU ENJOY A LARGE AREA OF THE ABALONE PEARL'S PEACOCK BLUES AND GREENS.

EARRINGS

EARRINGS ARE EASY TO DESIGN AND QUICK TO CONSTRUCT. IN ONLY A FEW MINUTES, IT'S POSSIBLE TO THROW TOGETHER A PAIR OF EARRINGS TO MATCH THE DRESS YOU PLAN TO WEAR THAT EVENING. SELECT A FEW BEADS, PUT THEM ON A HEADPIN, MAKE A LOOP, ATTACH AN EARWIRE, AND HOLD UP A PERFECTLY FINISHED PIECE OF JEWELRY.

1. To an eyepin (see "Using Headpins and Eyepins," page 126), add 1 gold bead, 1 mother-of pearl bead, and 1 gold bead. Make a wire-wrapped loop (as described in "Wire Wrapping," page 127) and attach to the earwire.

2. Add a round pearl to a headpin and make a half-finished loop. Attach it to the eye of the eyepin and wrap to finish closing the loop. Make and attach 3 of these to each earring.

TOOLS
Round-Nosed Pliers, Flat-Nosed Pliers

MATERIALS

2 17 by 13mm composite abalone mother-of -pearl beads

6 4mm round white freshwater pearls

2 2" gold-filled eyepins

6 ¹/₂" gold-filled headpins with ball tip

4 2.5mm gold-filled round beads

2 vermeil earwires

30.
FAUX PEARL AND CHAIN EARRINGS

CONSIDERING THE IMMENSE SATISFACTION IT BRINGS, THIS
DESIGN SEEMS ALMOST CRIMINALLY SIMPLE . OF COURSE,
EARRINGS ARE SOMETIMES FAR MORE COMPLEX THAN THESE
AND CAN TAKE MORE TIME , BUT OF ALL THE TYPES OF JEWELRY,
THEY OFFER THE QUICKEST ROUTE TO INSTANT GRATIFICATION.

To a headpin (see "Using Headpins and Eyepins," page 126), add 1
faux pearl, and then make a simple loop to attach it to the end link of
a piece of the chain. Attach the earwire to the other end link of the
chain.

TOOLS
Round-Nosed Pliers, Flat-Nosed Pliers

MATERIALS

2 12mm faux pearls

2 1¹/₂" pieces of gold-filled cable
chain with 6-mm links

2 1" gold-filled headpins

2 vermeil earwires

31.
TAHITIAN PEARL EARRINGS

WHEN PAIRED SIMPLY WITH A LITTLE HEADDRESS OF SOLID GOLD
TO FORM A DROP SHAPE, THESE LOVELY EXAMPLES OF THE
TAHITIAN "BLACK" PEARL WORK PERFECTLY.

To a headpin (see "Using Headpins and Eyepins," page 126), add 1
pearl, 1 bead cap, and 1 round bead. Make a loop and attach it to the
earwire. Repeat, and you have your earrings.

TOOLS
Round-Nosed Pliers, Flat-Nosed Pliers

MATERIALS

2 10mm baroque Tahitian black pearls

2 6mm 18K gold bead caps

2 1" gold-filled headpins

2 2mm 18K gold round beads

2 18K gold earwires with decoration

32.
POTATO PEARL AND CHAIN EARRINGS

ANOTHER ENCHANTING ASPECT OF EARRINGS IS THE
OPPORTUNITY THEY GIVE YOU TO USE ALL THE ODDS AND ENDS
THAT REMAIN AFTER DESIGNING A NECKLACE. THERE ARE
ALWAYS A FEW BEADS LEFT; WHY NOT USE THEM TO MAKE A SET
OF MATCHING PEARL EARRINGS?

1. Make the dangles by adding 1 gold bead, 1 pearl, and 1 gold
   bead to a headpin (see "Using Headpins and Eyepins," page
   126). Finish by making a loop. Make 30 of these in a mixture of
   colors.

2. Cut 2 pieces from the long-and-short chain so that each has 4
   long links surrounding 3 short links. They should each be about
   1½ inch long.

3. Slip an earwire through an end loop of the chain so that it hangs
   from the loop.

4. Open a jump ring, and add 3 of the dangles. Hook the ring onto
   the other end of the chain and close.

5. Using 3 more jump rings, attach 3 dangles to each of the 3 short
   links in the chain. Make sure you add the jump rings to the same
   side of the chain each time.

6. Add 3 more dangles to a jump ring and attach to the loop of the
   earwire.

TOOLS
Wire Cutters, Round-Nosed Pliers,
Flat-Nosed Pliers

MATERIALS

30	5mm potato-shaped pearls in various dyed colors (about a third of a 16" multicolor strand)
60	2.5mm gold-filled round beads
4	inches of gold-filled "long-and-short" chain (with long links measuring about ⁵/₁₆ ")
10	4mm gold-filled jump rings
30	½" gold-filled headpins with ball tip
2	vermeil earwires

33.
ROUND PEARL AND CHAIN EARRINGS

THE CHAIN USED IN THIS DESIGN IS CALLED "LONG AND SHORT"
BECAUSE IT ALTERNATES ONE LONG LINK WITH ONE SHORT LINK.

1. Make the dangles by adding a pearl and silver bead to a headpin (see "Using Headpins and Eyepins," page 126), and then making a loop. Make 30 of these.

2. To complete and finish the earrings, follow the instructions in steps 2–6 for "Potato Pearl and Chain earrings" (page 90).

TOOLS
Round-Nosed Pliers, Flat-Nosed Pliers

MATERIALS

30	3mm round pearls in natural silver tones
30	2.5mm sterling silver round beads
4"	sterling silver long-and-short chain (with long links measuring about $5/16$")
10	3mm sterling silver jump rings
30	$1/2$" sterling silver headpins with ball tip
2	sterling silver earwires

34.
COIN PEARL AND CHAIN EARRINGS

COIN PEARLS ALLOW YOU TO MAKE EARRINGS THAT ARE BOTH
BIG AND ELEGANT—THEIR SVELTE SLIMNESS COUNTERBALANCES
THEIR BREADTH.

1. Cut the chain into two 1-inch pieces, two 1 $1/2$-inch pieces, and two 2-inch pieces.

2. Make the pearl pendants by adding 1 gold bead, 1 pearl, and 1 gold bead to a headpin and forming a loop (see "Using Headpins and Eyepins," page 126). Make 6 of these.

3. Open the loop of a pendant and attach it to the end of a 2-inch chain. Add another pendant to the end of a 1$1/2$-inch chain. Add another to the end of a 1-inch chain.

4. Open the loop of the earwire, and add the pendants by attaching the end link of the chain. Start with the 1$1/2$-inch chain, followed by the 2-inch chain and then the 1-inch chain.

TOOLS
Wire Cutters, Round-Nosed Pliers,
Flat-Nosed Pliers

MATERIALS

6	10mm white coin pearls
	9" gold-filled fine cable chain (with links measuring about 3mm)
12	2.5mm gold-filled round beads
6	1" gold-filled headpins with ball tip
2	gold-filled earwires with ball

35.
SEED PEARL EARRINGS

THESE TINY PEARLS ARE CAPTURED IN A MINIATURE ABACUS
THAT DISPLAYS THEM OF AS A BROAD RECTANGULAR PATCH OF
COLOR AND LUSTER.

1. Place the two spacer bars side by side on a flat surface.

2. Put a charlotte on a headpin, and then thread the head pin
    through the first hole of one of the spacer bars.

3. Add five 3-millimeter pearls, and put the head pin through the
    first hole of the other spacer bar.

4. Add a charlotte, and make a simple loop the same size as that
    of the eyepin.

5. Repeat this for the second, fourth, and fifth holes of the spacer
    bars, leaving the center holes empty.

6. Cut the head off of the 1½ inch headpin. Make a simple loop on
    the end the same size as the other loops you have made. Add a
    charlotte, and pass the pin through the center hole in the bottom of
    the second spacer bar (so all the loops are in the same direction).

7. Add five 3-millimeter pearls and pass the pin through the center
    hole of the top spacer bar.

8. Add a charlotte, the double daisy, a 4-millimeter pearl, a daisy,
    and a charlotte. Then finish off with a wire-wrapped loop and
    add the earwire.

9. Open the loops at the bottom, and add the silver balls.

TOOLS

Wire Cutters, Round-Nosed Pliers, Flat-Nosed
Pliers (pliers must have very narrow tips)

MATERIALS

50	3mm side-drilled potato-shaped pearls in natural gray lilac or peacock color
2	4mm side-drilled potato-shaped pearls in natural gray lilac or peacock color
22	size 13/0 silver-plated charlottes
2	3mm sterling silver daisy spacer beads
10	2mm silver balls with loops
4	12mm five-hole sterling silver spacer bars
2	3.5mm sterling silver double daisy spacer beads
8	¾" sterling silver headpins
2	1½" sterling silver headpins
2	sterling silver earwires

36.
COIN PEARL EARRINGS

YOU NEED VERY FINE-NOSED PLIERS TO CREATE THIS DESIGN—
AS WELL AS GOOD EYESIGHT AND A DEGREE OF MANUAL
DEXTERITY!

1. Cut the middle link of the chain making two 8-link pieces.

2. For dangles, add a charlotte to each headpin, a 3.5mm pearl,
    and another charlotte. Make a simple loop at the top.

3. Opening the loops, attach 7 dangles to each piece of chain by
    adding 3 to the bottom link and then 2 on each link above that.

4. Cut the wire into 2 equal pieces. Make a simple loop at one end
    and attach it to the top link of the chain. Add a coin pearl to the
    wire. Using the flat-nosed pliers to make a right angle, bend the
    wire about $^3/_8$" above the pearl. With the round-nosed pliers,
    bend the wire into a loop. Make 2 or 3 turns around the base of
    the loop and then bend the wire around the face of the pearl.
    There should be enough wire left over to make several final turns
    around the base of the bottom loop. For the second earring, wrap
    the wire in the opposite direction.

5. Add the earwires to the top loops.

TOOLS
Round-Nosed pliers, Flat-Nosed pliers

MATERIALS

2   7mm peach small coin pearls

14 3.5–4mm near-round pearls in peach,
    pink, or cream colors

28 size 13/0 gold-plated charlottes

1" gold-filled "Rolo" chain (about 19 links)

14" vermeil headpins with ball tip

3" 24-gauge gold-filled wire (half-hard)

2   gold-filled earwires

37.
BLUE-AND-GREEN PEARL EARRINGS

TOP-DRILLED PEARLS CAN ALSO BE USED ON A VERTICAL AXIS
TO CREATE AN INTERESTING OFFSET PATTERN.

To a headpin, add a silver bead, a blue pearl, three green pearls, and a
silver bead. Make a simple loop to attach to the earwire.

TOOLS
Wire Cutters, Round-Nosed Pliers, Flat-Nosed
Pliers

MATERIALS

2   dyed blue freshwater potato-shape
    pearls about 8–9mm in diameter

6   dyed green top-drilled teardrop pearls,
    approximately 6–5mm

4   2.5mm sterling silver round beads

2   1$^1/_2$" pieces of sterling silver long-and-
    short chain

2   1$^1/_2$" silver headpins with ball tip

2   sterling silver earwires

38. CHANDELIER EARRINGS

THIS DESIGN USES A SPECIALTY FINDING FOR CHANDELIER EARRINGS. THE FIVE LOOPS AT THE BOTTOM CREATE THE CHANDELIER EFFECT CAUSED BY THE HANGING PEARLS.

1. Cut the wire into 28 1-inch pieces.

2. Using a piece of wire, make a wire-wrapped loop and add a pearl. Make an unfinished loop at the other end of the wire. Attach it to the outside loop of the chandelier earring finding and finish the loop by wrapping. You will need very narrow-nosed flat pliers to finish the wrapping.

3. Attach another 4 pearls to the other chandelier loops in the same way.

4. Attach another pearl to each of the previous rows of pearls, using the wire pieces and the same wire-wrapping technique.

5. Attach another pearl to the middle three rows in the same manner.

6. Attach another pearl to the middle row in the same manner.

7. Attach a final pearl to each row by adding it to a headpin and making a wire-wrapped loop.

8. Add another pearl to a headpin and attach it to the inside loop of the chandelier earring finding.

TOOLS
Wire Cutters, Round-Nosed Pliers, Flat-Nosed Pliers

MATERIALS

40	3mm white potato-shaped pearls
2	16–27mm vermeil chandelier earring findings
12	$1/2$" vermeil headpins with ball tip
28"	26-gauge gold-filled wire
2	gold-filled earwires with ball

39.
HORIZONTAL STICK PEARL EARRINGS

THE SIZE OF A SINGLE PEARL IS JUST ABOUT AS BIG AS YOU WANT
AN EARRING TO BE, SO STICK PEARLS ARE GREAT CHOICES.

1. Start by making the 6 dangles. Add to a headpin one spacer, a zircon, and another spacer, and then make a loop.

2. Put a stick pearl on a headpin, and make a loop at the end without the ball tip. Turn it so that the pearl is sitting on the loop. Now make a semi-finished loop at the top. Slip it through the loop of the earwire, and wrap the tail of the headpin under the loop so that the little ball at the tip comes to rest at the top of the pearl. (In this way, the gold ball creates a little drop of gold on the pearl, forming an integral part of the design.)

3. Open the jump ring, and use it to attach three dangles to the bottom loop of the headpin.

TOOLS
Wire Cutters, Round-Nosed Pliers,
Flat-Nosed Pliers

MATERIALS
2 20mm stick pearls
6 4mm faceted natural zircon rondels
12 3mm vermeil daisy spacer beads
2 3mm gold-filled ring
8 $^1/_2$" gold-filled headpins with ball tip
2 vermeil earwires with decoration

40.
VERTICAL STICK PEARL EARRINGS

1. Cut the long headpin about $^5/_8$ inch longer than the pearl. Put it through the pearl and make a loop at the end without the ball. Following step 2 for the Horizontal Stick Pearl Earrings (above), let the pearl rest on the loop and create another at the top to attach the earwire. Twist the tail of the wire so the ball rests at top of the pearl.

2. To a headpin, add 1 bead cap, 1 pearl, 1 bead cap, and 1 round bead. Make a loop and attach to the bottom loop of the stick pearl.

TOOLS
Wire Cutters, Round-Nosed Pliers,
Flat-Nosed Pliers

MATERIALS
2 20mm stick pearls
2 7mm coral beads
2 2.5mm gold-filled round beads
4 5mm vermeil bead caps
2 3mm gold-filled rings
2 $^1/_2$" and two $1^1/_2$" gold-filled headpins with ball tip
2 gold-filled earwires with decoration

41.
KESHI PEARL LARIAT

THESE TWO NECKLACES HAVE THE SAME DESIGN BUT USE
PEARLS AND SPACER BEADS IN DIFFERENT SHAPES. VARYING THE
INGREDIENTS IN ANY OF THESE DESIGNS GIVES YOU A PIECE OF
JEWELRY THAT IS UNIQUELY YOURS.

1. Attach the beading wire to the ring using the crimp bead (see
   "Using Crimp Beads to Attach Clasps," page 124). Add the crimp
   cover. Add 1 large gold bead and 1 pearl. The sequence of beads
   is random, so you feel free to create your own version. If you
   want to replicate the exact design from the photo on page 98,
   follow this pattern (see abbreviations in ingredients list):
   - d, 3r, d, p, d, r
   - d, p, d, r, large gold bead
   - r, d, p, d, r, f, r, f, r, large gold bead
   - r, f, p, f, r, f, p, d, 8r, large gold bead, p, r
   - f, p (repeated a total of 4 times), f, r
   - f, p (repeated a total of 3 times), large gold bead, p, f, r
   - f, p (repeated a total of 6 times)
   - f, d, 3r, f, r, f, r, d, p, f,
   - p, 3f, p, f, r, f, p, f, p, d, r, d, p
   - Large gold bead, p, d, r, large gold bead, r, d, p, large gold
     bead, and a crimp bead

2. To make the loop, add the following pattern after the crimp: 7 r,
   d, r, f, 8r, f, r, f, r, f, 2r, f. Pass the wire back through the crimp and
   the large gold bead. Close the crimp and snip off the remaining
   wire as close to the gold bead as possible.

3. Make 10 little dangles with the assorted gemstones and small
   round gold beads. Make 6 of them by adding 1 gemstone and 1
   gold bead to a headpin. Make 2 more using a combination of 1
   gemstone, 1 gold bead, 1 gemstone, and 1 gold bead. Make the
   final 2 dangles with a arrangement of 1 gemstone and 3 gold
   beads. Hook all the dangles onto the bottom of the gold ring,
   where you started the lariat, by opening and closing the loops.

TOOLS
Crimping Pliers, Wire Cutters,
Round-Nosed Pliers

TO MAKE A 21-INCH LARIAT

29 large keshi pearls about 14mm in size,
   about a 16" strand (abbreviated as "p" in
   recipe)

51 4mm hand-cut faceted ruby rondels,
   about half a 16" strand (abbreviated as
   "r" in recipe)

8 9mm gold-filled hollow round beads

15 4mm gold-filled daisy spacer beads
   (abbreviated as "d" in recipe)

34 2mm gold-filled faceted beads
   (abbreviated as "f" in recipe)

1 5mm gold-filled soldered ring

10 assorted 4mm gemstone beads in red
   tones for the end tassel

6 2mm and six 3mm gold-filled round
   beads for the end tassel

10 $\frac{1}{2}$" gold-filled headpins with ball tip for
   the end tassel

2 gold-filled crimp beads

2 gold crimp covers

26 inches of beading wire

42.
COIN PEARL LARIAT

USE THE INGREDIENTS ON THE FACING PAGE, BUT SUBSTITUTE
COIN PEARLS FOR THE KESHI. I HAVE ALSO SUBSTITUTED 5
MILLIMETER BI-CONE GOLD BEADS FOR EACH OF THE LARGE
GOLD BEADS. OF COURSE, I HAVE MADE A FEW ARRANGEMENT
CHANGES TO THE RANDOM PATTERN, BUT THEN THAT IS THE
WHOLE POINT OF A RANDOM PATTERN – IT MAKES EVERY PIECE
OF JEWELRY UNIQUE.

1. Attach the beading wire to the ring using the crimp bead. Add a
   crimp cover. Then add a gold bi-cone bead and a pearl. The
   sequence of beads is random, but if you want to continue with
   the design shown on page 99, follow this pattern (see
   abbreviations in ingredients list):
   - d, 3r, d, p, d, r
   - d, p, d, r, bi-cone bead
   - r, d, p, d, r, f, r, f, r, bi-cone bead
   - r, f, p, f, r, f, p, d, 8r, bi-cone bead, p, r
   - f, p (repeated a total of 4 times), f, r
   - f, p (repeated a total of 3 times), bi-cone bead, p, f, r
   - f, p (repeated a total of 6 times)
   - f, d, 3r, f, r, f, r, d, p, t
   - p, 3f, p, f, r, f, p, f, p, d, r, d, p
   - Bi-cone bead, p, d, r, bi-cone bead, r, d, p, bi-cone bead,
     and a crimp bead

TOOLS
Wire Cutters, Round-Nosed Pliers,
Flat-Nosed Pliers

MATERIALS
29	14mm coin pearls, 16" strand (abbreviated as "p" in the recipe)
51	4mm hand-cut facetted ruby rondels, about half a 16" strand (abbreviated as "r" in recipe)
8	5mm gold-filled hollow bicone beads
15	4mm gold-filled daisy spacer beads (abbreviated as "d" in the recipe)
34	2mm gold filled facetted beads (abbreviated as "f" in the recipe)
1	5mm gold-filled soldered ring
10	assorted 4mm gemstone beads in red tones for the end tassel
6	2mm and six 3mm gold-filled round beads for the end tassel
10"	gold-filled headpins with ball tip for the end tassel
22	gold-filled crimp beads
26"	beading wire

43.
PEARL "BERRIES" BRACELET

THE FANCIFUL NAME OF THIS DESIGN COMES FROM ITS MANY DANGLING PIECES, WHICH LOOK A LITTLE LIKE BERRIES ON A VINE. THE TECHNIQUE FOR MAKING THE BERRIES MAY SEEM HARD AT FIRST, BUT IS ACTUALLY QUITE SIMPLE ONCE YOU GET THE HANG OF IT, AND IT CAN BE USED FOR OTHER DESIGNS.

1. To make the berries, start by adding a round bead to a headpin. Then add a bead cap with the concave side facing up. Add 1 pearl. Add another bead cap, this time with the concave side facing down. Add another round bead. Use your round-nosed pliers to grip the headpin about $\frac{1}{4}$ inch above the bead. Make a loop and wrap the tail of the head pin between the bottom of the loop and the top of the bead (see "Using Headpins and Eyepins," page 126).

2. When you have made all the berries, use a split ring to attach the lobster clasp to the flat cable chain.

3. Open a jump ring. Slip on 3 pearl berries in different colors. Attach the jump ring with the "berry cluster" to the second link down from the clasp. Close it around the link. (See "Using Jump Rings and Split Rings," page 125.)

4. Make another berry cluster (as explained in step 3) and attach it to the chain two links down from the first cluster. **You must be very careful to attach all the clusters to the same side of the chain. Hold the chain straight after you add a cluster to make sure it's hanging on the same side as the first.** Now make and add the rest of the clusters, attaching them to every other link ot the chain and making sure they are on the same side of the link as the rest. Your last cluster should end on the last chain link. If it does not, check to make sure it fits around your wrist, and then snip off any excess links.

TOOLS
Wire Cutters, Round-Nosed Pliers, Flat-Nosed Pliers

MATERIALS

52	5.5mm freshwater potato-shaped pearls, in various natural and dyed colors (about three-quarters of a 16" multicolor strand)
52	1" 24-gauge gold-filled headpins
104	2.5mm gold-filled round beads
104	5mm gold-filled bead caps
14	5mm oval gold-filled jump rings
7	$\frac{1}{2}$" gold-filled cable chain with 8mm links
1	11mm gold-filled lobster clasp
1	5mm gold-filled split ring

NOTE
The clasp of this bracelet can be attached to whichever link offers the best fit. If you have a narrow wrist, use the link closest to the last bead, then a cluster or two can dangle down from the clasp.

44.
PEARL SILVER BRACELET

SURROUNDING THESE PEARLS WITH SILVER BEADS INCREASES THE GEM'S SILVER HUE. LARGE SPACER BEADS MAKE THE PEARLS LOOK ALMOST AS THOUGH THEY ARE SET IN A BAND OF SILVER. THE PENDANT AND THE MOONSTONE CLASP MAKE THIS DESIGN ATTRACTIVE EVEN WHEN IT TURNS ON YOUR WRIST.

1. First, make the little pendant that will hang beside the bracelet clasp. To the headpin, add 1 pearl, 1 star-shaped silver bead, and 1 round silver bead. Make a small loop to finish it off.

2. Using a crimp bead, attach the beading wire to the tongue end of the clasp. Now add 3 of the 4 millimeter daisy spacers, 1 pearl, and 1 of the star-shaped silver beads. Repeat this pattern until you have used all the pearls or reached a length of about 6¹/₂ inches. Check the bracelet around your wrist. If the length fits, add 1 round silver bead, the pendant, and a crimp. If it is too short, repeat the pattern and measure again. When it fits comfortably around the wrist, atttach to the main part of the box clasp, and add the crimp covers.

USING COLOR

THE DESIGNS ON THESE TWO PAGES SHOW TWO WAYS OF TREATING COLOR IN PEARL JEWELRY. THE COMPLEMENTARY COLOR OF THE BEADS SUPPORTS AND ENHANCES THE COLOR OF THE PEARLS. THE EYEGLASS-LEASH DESIGN USES THE NEUTRAL WHITE OF THE PEARLS TO EMPHASIZE THE TINY SPECKS OF TURQUOISE AND INCREASE THEIR IMPACT.

TOOLS

Wire Cutters, Crimping Pliers, Round-Nose Pliers

MATERIALS

19	6mm near-round freshwater pearls with a silver hue
10	3–7mm star-shaped sterling silver beads
27	4mm sterling silver daisy spacer beads
2	sterling silver crimp beads
2	sterling silver crimp bead covers
2	2.5mm sterling silver round beads
1	sterling silver head pin with a cubic zircon stud
1	box clasp with moonstone inset
12"	beading wire

45.
RUBY AND PEARL BRACELET

THE PURPLE SILK THREAD AND THE PURPLE-RED RUBIES DEEPEN
THE PURPLE TONES OF THE LARGE PEARLS IN THIS STUNNING
BRACELET.

1. Double the thread, and attach half the clasp using the clamshell
    bead tip (see "Using Bead Tips to Attach Clasps," page 116).
    Make a knot after the bead tip, then string on 1 ruby rondel.
    Make another knot, then string on 1 pearl (see "Getting
    Knotted," page 114). Continue alternating rubies with pearls,
    being sure to knot after each one. Periodically check the size
    around your wrist. When the length fits around it comfortably,
    finish off by using the bead tip to attach the thread to the other
    half of the clasp.

TOOLS
Beading Needle, Awl, Flat-Nosed Pliers,
Scissors

MATERIALS

11 10mm near-round freshwater pearls with
    natural purple hue

12 4mm faceted ruby rondels

2 gold-filled clamshell bead tips

1 gold-filled box clasp

3 ft of size F purple silk embroidery thread

46.
PEARL AND TURQUOISE EYEGLASS LEASH

THE COLOR OF THE PEARLS IN THIS DESIGN GIVES THE
SCATTERING OF TINY TURQUOISE BEADS AN IMPACT COMPLETELY
DISPROPORTIONATE TO THEIR SIZE.

1. Start by making the little dangles that will hang beside the
   clasp. To a headpin, add 1 pearl and 1 turquoise bead. Finish it
   off with a small loop (see "Using Headpins and Eyepins," page
   126). Make 6 of these dangles.

2. Using 1 crimp bead and 2 silver round beads, attach the beading
   wire to one of the clasps (see "Using Bead Tips to Attach
   Clasps," page 116). Add 3 pearls and 1 turquoise bead. Repeat
   this pattern until the strand is about 23 inches long. Add 2 silver
   round beads and a crimp, and attach to the other clasp. Add the
   crimp covers.

3. Open a jump ring, and slip on 3 of the dangles. Hook the jump
   ring onto the loop of a clasp and close (see "Using Jump Rings
   and Split Rings," page 125). Repeat this for the other clasp. Use
   the spring ring clasps to hook the chain onto each loop of the
   eyeglass holder. To use the chain as a necklace, unhook it from
   the eyeglass holder and hook one clasp to the other. You can
   also attach small rubber eyeglass holders to the clasps for a
   different style of leash.

TOOLS
Wire Cutters, Crimping Pliers, Round-Nosed
Pliers

MATERIALS FOR A 24-INCH LEASH
22"	2–3mm side-drilled white potato-shaped pearls
70	1.5mm reconstituted turquoise beads
4	2.5mm round sterling silver beads
2	4mm sterling silver jump rings
2	sterling silver crimp beads
2	sterling silver crimp bead covers
6	sterling silver head pins with ball tip
2	6mm sterling silver spring ring clasps
1	sterling silver eyeglass holder
28"	beading wire

THE MAKING OF A GEM

UNLESS THEY COME FROM YOUR GRANDMOTHER'S NECKLACE, IT IS A VIRTUAL CERTAINTY THAT ANY PEARL YOU ACQUIRE WILL HAVE BEEN MADE WITH A LITTLE HUMAN ASSISTANCE. THE SUPPLY OF NATURAL PEARLS GATHERED FROM "WILD" OYSTERS NOW COMPRISES A TINY FRACTION OF THE PEARL MARKET.

Whether they grow in sea or fresh water, almost all of today's pearls are farmed. Many gemologists and experts in jewelry valuation still stubbornly insist that the products of these farms be called "cultured pearls" rather than "pearls." But these specialists are fighting a rearguard action. The world in general has already decided that farmed pearls are just dandy and has taken to calling the cultured gems simply "pearls," while the unassisted variety are distinguished as "natural pearls." And it is difficult to find fault with this. After all, both types of pearl are produced by the same animal, and the cultured variety looks to all outward appearances the same as a natural pearl. The difference, all on the inside, is of little concern to the average pearl buyer.

Pearls are unique among gems in that they are grown in animals rather than dug out of the earth. Until the early twentieth century, the animals performed this task with no particular interference from man. The certainty of a steadily declining supply of wild pearls, however, promised great profit to those who could solve the puzzle of how to encourage mollusks to make pearls on demand. It had been known for hundreds of years that some mollusks could be induced to coat alien objects with their precious nacre. The Chinese, for instance, practiced a method of placing shaped objects or smooth hemispheres between the mantle and the shell of freshwater mussels. This would produce "blister" pearls, which could be cut out of the shell and set in jewelry. Creating the classic round pearl for necklaces was a knottier problem, one that was finally solved in Japan.

Although Kokichi Mikimoto was not the first to culture round pearls, his dedication and drive made him the father of the cultured pearl industry. The son of a noodle maker, Mikimoto spent his entire life perfecting the art of inducing the Japanese pearl oyster to make his

PEARL CULTIVATION

The South Sea pearl is widely cultured, especially in Australia. Here, the giant *Pinctada maxima* is taken from the wild. Carefully nucleated, they are then carried hundreds of miles to a new home and nurtured with enormous care in pristine deep water. The pearls are big, beautiful, and suitably expensive. Huge sums of money are invested in the production of South Sea pearls. The Paspaley company, a family pearling business that has its activities spread over the coast of Northern Australia, maintains a highly sophisticated operation linked together by a modern fleet of ships and aircraft. Far from its beginnings as a handful of individual divers, it is now a large corporation that has placed a major bet on pearls retaining their historic value for many years to come.

The islands of Tahiti also continue to nurture their very special "black" pearls, which have become prized for their iridescence and large size.

product, and then promoting the virtues of these pearls all over the world. Around the turn of the last century, a Japanese biologist and a carpenter each independently discovered the way to culture a pearl. They inserted a piece of the epithelial membrane (the lip of mantle tissue) into a mollusk's body along with a small round bead. The reaction of the creature was to create a sack around the intruding object and start coating it with nacre.

Mikimoto, who already had patents to produce pearl shapes, adapted this method (called Mise-Niskikawa) to produce round cultured pearls and made Japan dominant in the commercial pearl market for the rest of the twentieth century. Part of the secret of Mikimoto's Japanese pearls was his discovery of the very best "seed" to place in the mollusk—ironically, this turned out to be a bead made from the shell of an American freshwater mussel. Even today, a little bit of America lies at the heart of most Japanese and many other cultured pearls.

While the method of culturing pearls sounds simple, it is not. It depends on highly skilled technicians, called nucleators, who are able to perform minor surgery on the mollusk in order to implant the nucleus in such a way that it causes no harm. The Japanese guarded their process and instruments closely and forced all players in other countries to pay for their technology and their skills.

For many years, the name "Mikimoto" was synonymous with fine cultured pearls. When other Japanese producers joined in the industry, it was the Japanese name for the mollusk *Pinctada fucata* that would become renowned: Akoya pearls became the byword for quality all over the world. The Japanese took another step forward when they started culturing freshwater pearls in Lake Biwa, near Kyoto. So dominant were these pearls that until a few years ago, many people erroneously referred to all freshwater pearls as Biwas.

The insatiable demands of the pearl-buying public, along with the environmental stress of trying to produce so many pearls in such a small area, ensured that the Japanese could not keep their grip on the business forever. Although still a major player in the distribution of pearls, the Japanese have now lost their monopoly on production. Besides China, there are now fully independent pearl producers in Tahiti, Australia, Indonesia, the Philippines, and even the United States, home of that critical Mississippi mussel that lies at the heart of most cultured round pearls.

THE "AGRICULTURE" OF PEARLS

The future of large-scale pearl production seems to lie in China. Here, freshwater pearls are produced with no solid nucleus at all, just a piece of mantle tissue. These non-nucleated pearls are all nacre and can hardly be distinguished from natural pearls. If you travel through certain parts of the Chinese countryside, you might notice a strange sight: large ponds with surfaces patterned by a graph-like series of dots. On closer inspection, these turn out to be empty plastic bottles, each attached by a string to a growing mussel several feet beneath the surface. These bottles start out lying flat on the water's surface. As the mussel grows and exerts more weight on the neck, the bottle is dragged down into an upright position, and the farmer knows it is time to harvest his crop. This might not be not quite as romantic a picture as the images of scantily clad pearl divers gathering wild oysters from the depths of the sea, but it is the reality that has made it possible for all of us to indulge in the delight of pearl jewelry, rather than having to save up for that one single strand of expensive pearls.

JEWELRY

TECHNIQUES

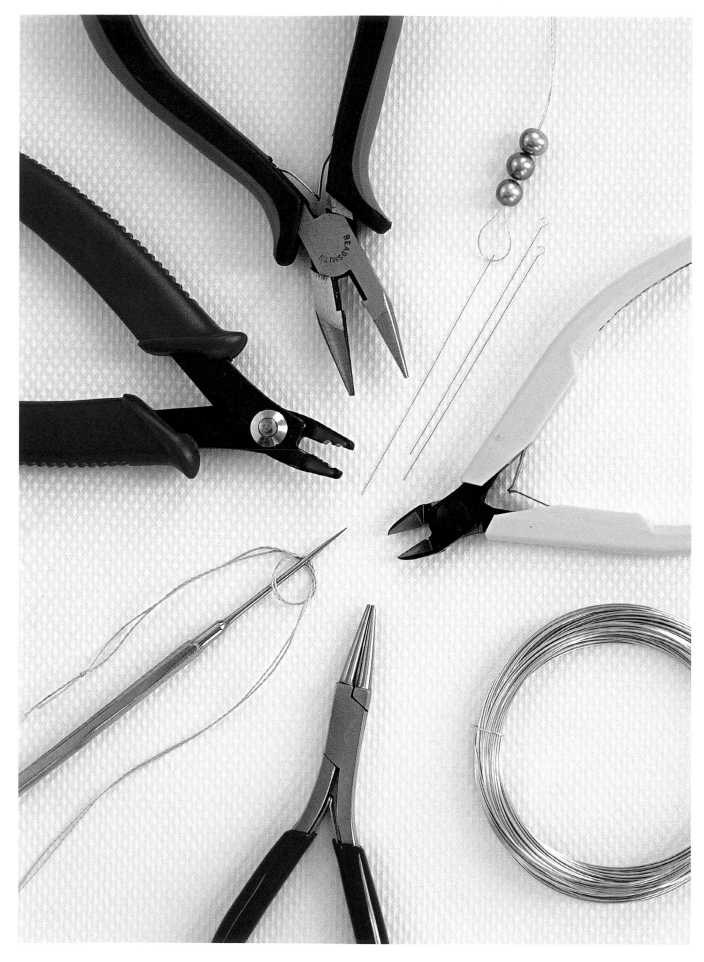

BASIC JEWELRY MAKING

The following pages describe the techniques used to make the designs in this book. These are the methods that have worked best for me in my many years as a jewelry maker. More importantly, I have found that they work well for the people I have taught and for the thousands of people who have been taught by our Beadworks instructors.

Some of these techniques are very simple and require hardly any practice, although dexterity is a big help. Others need patience and several or many attempts to get right. If you find yourself becoming frustrated, remember that this work is mostly a matter of familiarity. If at first you don't succeed, cut the pearls off the thread or wire and start all over again! There are also many bead stores and educational organizations that offer beading classes. If you learn best through hands-on teaching, this is a good, quick way to get started.

In order to begin working with beads, you need a well-lit, flat, hard surface with some kind of soft covering that will keep the beads from rolling around. If you plan to work at a table or desk, you can buy bead mats or bead design boards, or simply use a towel. I prefer to work on my studio floor, which is well carpeted and allows me to surround myself with tools and beads (and a cat to keep me company). Keep a mirror nearby so that you can check the look and length of your necklaces and earrings.

Good tools make everything a lot easier. I always use two pairs of flat-nosed pliers, one of them with very narrow jaws. Round-nosed pliers should have tips narrow enough to make very small loops. If you discover you have a love for making jewelry, treat yourself to a truly high-quality pair of wire-cutters. Once you are seriously into making jewelry, you'll find that lots of little containers are absolutely essential for storing your beads and findings. These can be anything from old jars to specialized bead vials, but it does help if they are transparent and have lids. Multicompartment plastic boxes are also a great storage method. But don't worry about accumulating lots of tools and gadgets in the beginning. Pick one of the easier designs, and just get started!

THE GOLDEN RULES

The carpenter's maxim is "Measure twice, cut once." The wise necklace maker measures at least twice, tries it around the neck for size, and then sets it down to check the pattern. Never finish off until you are absolutely sure that the length is correct.

Don't let a little clumsy work spoil the whole piece. If you forgive a bad knot or a missed spacer, you will see the flaw every time you wear the jewelry. It's better to start over and get it right.

Don't ruin good ingredients by mixing them in with poor ones. Even if the material will be hidden by the beads, or under your hair at the back of your neck, use high-quality materials. (Never, ever string anything on fishing line!)

Assume you are going to make mistakes—I constantly make mistakes even after many, many, many years of jewelry making. If the recipe calls for two headpins, understand you will need at least two more on standby, for when you cut them too short or bend them too badly. If it requires 20 inches of beading wire, make sure you have the rest of the spool nearby in case you need to start all over again.

Don't waste time looking for the exact bead called for in the recipe. Use a substitute of the same quality with similar design values (color, size, shape, texture).

I.
GETTING KNOTTED: THE ART OF USING SILK THREAD

Strands of pearls are traditionally strung on silk thread, which is thought to offer the best compromise between strength and flexibility. It is best to thread the pearls onto a doubled strand of silk, both to add strength and increase the size of the knots. While you can use silk thread without knotting between each pearl, it is traditional to make these knots in order to highlight each pearl and to prevent them from chafing against each other.

STRINGING ON SILK THREAD

You need a needle to draw the thread through the pearls. While any thin needle will do, flexible twisted wire needles make the job a lot easier.

1. Thread the silk through the eye of the needle and draw it through until the doubled length is enough for the necklace (Illus. A). If you are knotting between each pearl, your doubled strand should be at least twice as long as the finished necklace. For example, an 18-inch knotted necklace will require two yards, or 72 inches, of silk thread. If you are not knotting between each bead, the doubled thread should be about 6 inches longer than the finished piece. An 18-inch necklace will therefore require 4 feet, or 48 inches, of thread.

2. Tie the doubled end of the thread with a simple overhand knot (Illus. B). Pull on the tail with your pliers to tighten the knot.

3. To tighten the knot even more, separate the two threads and pull apart (Illus. C).

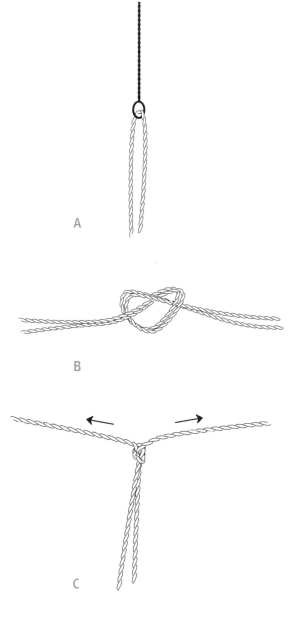

A

B

C

USING AN AWL TO MAKE KNOTS

An awl is a metal needle with a long handle that is used for getting knots to sit snugly against beads or bead tips. It is very simple to use once you know how. You can use the next step to practice knotting. Once you begin to make a real necklace, you will first have to attach the clasp (see pages 116–121).

1. Add a pearl or bead to the thread. Make an overhand knot anywhere along the thread, but do not tighten it. Put the point of the awl through the knot, and gently reduce the size of the knot until it fits loosely around the awl (Illus. A). Put your finger on the thread so that the knot lies between your finger and the awl.

2. Keeping your finger on the knot, move the awl toward the bead. You should be able to easily move the knot all the way down the thread until it lies snugly against the bead (Illus. A).

3. Once you have the knot in position, slowly remove the awl as you pull on the thread to tighten the knot (Illus. B).

4. To tighten the knot even more, you can separate the two threads and pull them apart to help force the knot closer to the pearl (Illus. C).

5. Add another bead and push it firmly against the knot you have just made. Make another knot as described in steps 1–3. Make sure the beads lie snugly against one another. Continue practicing with a few beads until you are confident that you have the technique mastered.

TOOLS TIPS

When you need to knot and can't find your awl, fold out a safety pin and use that.

If you've lost your scissors or can't find your cutters, get out your nail clippers. They are usually very sharp and you can get them nice and close to your bead to cut off excess thread or wire.

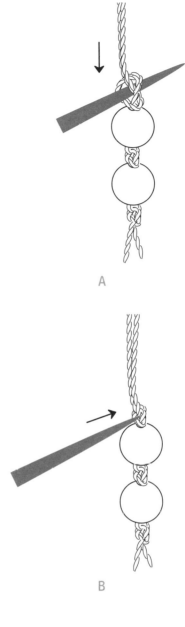

A

B

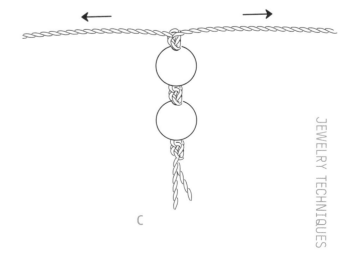

C

II.
USING BEAD TIPS TO ATTACH CLASPS

When stringing on silk thread (see "Getting Knotted" on page 114), you need to finish off the ends in a way that will let you attach them to the two halves of a clasp. The little findings that enable you to do this are called bead tips. One end of a bead tip is a simple loop that will connect to the clasp. The other end grips the knot at the end of your thread.

To use either kind of bead tip, start with your thread doubled and knotted at the end.

TO USE STRING-THROUGH CLAMSHELL BEAD TIPS

1. Make another overhand knot on top of the first knot at the end of your doubled thread. This is easier to do if you use your awl to guide the loop of the second knot so it sits on the first. Tighten that knot as well. Unless you are very sure of your knots, add a dab of hypo-cement (a clear glue with a precision applicator) or clear nail polish. Trim off the excess tail of the thread with a pair of sharp scissors (Illus. A, B, C, D).

2. Pass your needle and thread into the open clamshell of the bead tip and through the hole at the base of the shell. Pull the thread completely through so that the knot sits snugly inside the clamshell. Using flat-nosed pliers, gently squeeze the sides of the shell together so that it closes around the knot and grips it firmly (Illus. E, F).

3. Make another single knot tight against the bottom of the bead tip. Now add the beads to the length of the silk thread to create your necklace.

4. Once you have finished stringing all the beads of your necklace, finish it off by passing the needle and thread through the hole on the outside of another bead tip. (Remember to make a knot after the last pearl.)

5. Pull the thread so that the last knot of your necklace sits firmly against the outside of the bead tip. Now tie an overhand knot so that it sits inside the clamshell of the bead tip. To position the knot properly, use your awl to move the loop of the knot as close to the inside wall of the bead tip as possible. Tighten the knot, pulling the awl out at the last moment.

6. Make a second overhand knot, and tighten it on top of the first. Add a dab of hypo-cement if needed. Using flat-nosed pliers, gently squeeze the sides of the shell together so that it closes around the knot and grips it firmly. Using a sharp pair of scissors, trim off the rest of the thread as close to the outside of the bead tip as possible.

7. You now have a strand with a bead tip at either end. Put the open loop of one bead tip through the ring on one half of the clasp. Use flat-nosed pliers to close the loop so that it is firmly attached to the ring. Attach the other bead tip to the other part of the clasp in the same manner.

TIP

If you add a few smaller beads to the beginning and end of your necklace, it will be easier to open and undo the clasp when you wear it.

QUICK TRICK

If you have an idea for a necklace but don't have the time to make it up, string a few beads defining at least part of the design on a piece of thread or even fishing line and tie off both ends. This way, you will be able to remember what the idea was when you find time to make it.

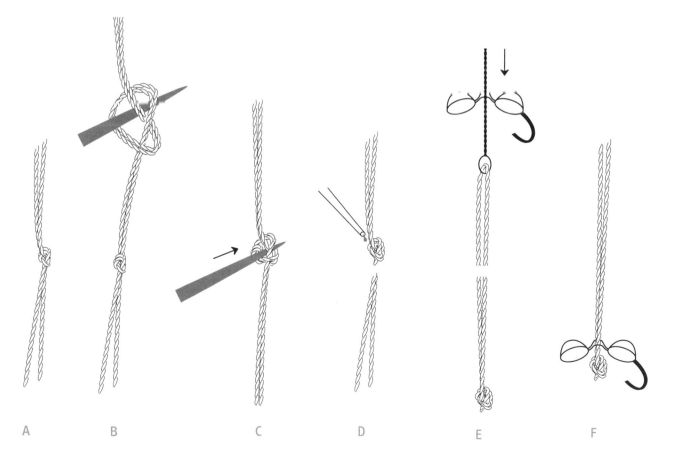

A   B   C   D   E   F

USING BASKET BEAD TIPS

While it is a little more difficult to make the final knot using this style
of bead tip, basket beads give a more sophisticated look to your
jewelry—if you can master the technique.

1. Take the end of the doubled thread and tie a simple overhand
    knot. Tighten it by gripping the tail with pliers and pulling. Trim
    off the excess tail of the thread with a pair of sharp scissors
    (Illus. A).

2. Pass your needle and thread into the basket and through the
    hole at its bottom. Pull the thread completely through so that the
    knot sits snugly inside the bottom of the basket. Put a tiny dab of
    hypo-cement or clear nail polish on the knot (Illus. B, C, D).

3. Make another overhand knot near the outside of the bead tip,
    and use your awl to move the loop of that knot tight against the
    bottom of the basket. This knot keeps the beads from chafing
    against the bead tip and improve the overall appearance.

4. Now add the beads to the silk thread to create your necklace
    (Illus. E).

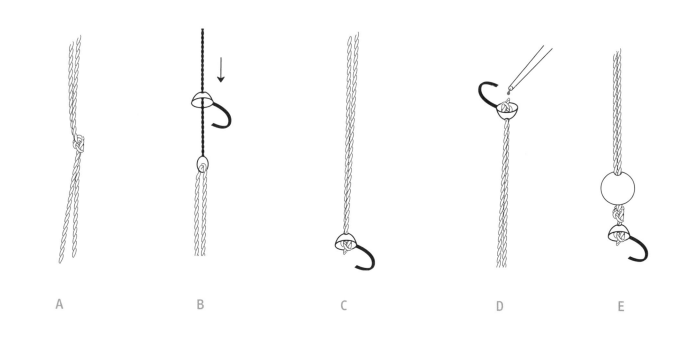

A   B   C   D   E

5. Once you have completed stringing all the beads of your necklace, make an overhand knot, and use the awl to position it tightly against the last bead. Pass the needle and thread through the hole on the outside bottom of another basket bead tip. Pull the thread until the bead tip sits firmly against the knot after the last bead (Illus. F).

6. Tie an overhand knot, and use your awl to move the loop of the knot as close as possible to the bottom inside wall of the bead tip (Illus. G). Tighten the knot, pulling the awl out at the last moment. It takes a little practice to get this final knot to slip into the basket, but it is important to get a good tight fit so that no thread can be seen once the necklace is complete. Add a tiny dab of hypo-cement or clear nail polish to firmly secure this knot (Illus. H).

7. Finish off by attaching the ends of the bead tips to the clasp as above (Illus. I + J).

F   G   H   I   J

III.
USING FRENCH WIRE
TO ATTACH CLASPS

French wire is a kind of flexible metal sheath that covers part of the silk thread so that it can be attached directly to the clasp.

1.   Thread the silk on the needle and knot the end.

2.   Thread on 3 pearls and a $1/4$-inch piece of French wire (Illus. A).

3.   Pass the needle through the loop of the clasp and back through the pearl nearest the French wire. Use flat-nosed pliers to pull the needle through first. Then grip the thread just behind the needle and pull the rest of the thread through. As you pull the thread, watch to make sure that the French wire gathers up into a tight loop around the clasp (Illus. B, C).

4.   When the pearl lies snugly against both ends of the French wire, make a knot on the other side by forming a loop and passing the needle through. Tighten this knot against the pearl (Illus. D).

5.   Now pass the needle the through the next pearl. Slide the pearl tight against the knot you have just made, and make another knot on the other side (Illus. E).

6.   Pass the needle the through the last pearl. Slide it tight against the knot you have just made, and make another knot on the other side (Illus. F).

7.   Cut away the tail and very end knot of the thread, and put a tiny dab of hypo-cement on the knot you have just made (Illus. G).

8.   Finish stringing and knotting all of your pearls until the third pearl from the end. Add the last three pearls to the necklace without putting knots between them (Illus. H).

9.   Add $1/4$ inch of French wire, and pass the needle through the loop of the other half of the clasp (llus. I).

TIP

Using French wire requires a little practice and patience. If the holes in the pearls are small, then you should use the thinner size E thread. You can also use a smaller size 6 needle, if necessary.

10. Pass the needle through the loop of the clasp and back through the pearl nearest the French wire. As you pull the thread, watch to make sure that the French wire gathers up into a tight loop around the clasp (llus. J).

11. Make a knot on the other side by forming a loop and passing the needle through. Tighten this knot against the pearl (llus. K).

12. Pass the needle the through the next pearl and make another knot on the other side (llus. L).

13. Pass the needle through the third pearl. Pull the thread very taut, and cut it away as close to the pearl as possible. Use a very sharp-pointed pair of scissors or cutters to get in as close as possible. The ends of the thread should be hidden by the pearl (llus. M).

14. Add a dab of hypo-cement or clear nail polish to the last two knots you made (llus. N).

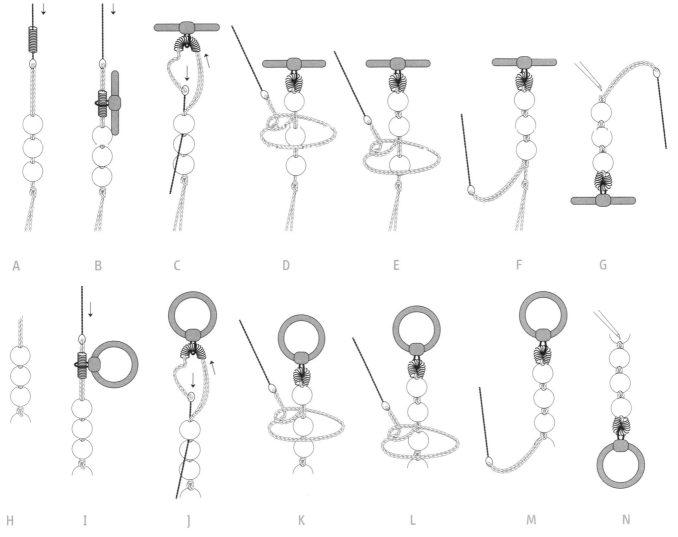

A   B   C   D   E   F   G

H   I   J   K   L   M   N

IV.
MAKING A
CONTINUOUS
STRAND (NO CLASP)

If a necklace is big enough to fit comfortably over your head, it does not need a clasp. This continuous strand method can be used for opera and rope lengths (those measuring at least 30 inches).

1. Double your thread through the needle and tie a knot about six inches from the end. This extra long tail will make it easy for you to grip and tighten the thread as you work.

2. Add three pearls without knotting (Illus. A). Make another knot 2 inches above these pearls (leaving 2 inches of thread empty).

3. Add the rest of your pearls, knotting between each one (Illus. B). Make a knot after the last pearl.

4. Insert your needle into the outside of the very first pearl you started with (that is, the end near the long tail of thread). Pull the needle through and tighten so that all the pearls lie together, with the first three pearls moving up to rest beside the second knot you made (Illus. C).

5. Once the thread is taut and all the pearls are together in a continuous circle, make a knot between the first and second pearl using the loop method described in step 4 on page 120, disregarding the reference to French wire (Illus. D).

6. Pass the needle through the second pearl. Tighten the thread, and make another knot (Illus. E).

7. Pass the needle through the third pearl. Pull the thread very taut, and cut it off as close to the pearl as possible. The tail of the thread should end up hidden in the third pearl. Add a tiny dab of hypo-cement to the knots between the first and second pearls and the second and third pearls (Illus. F).

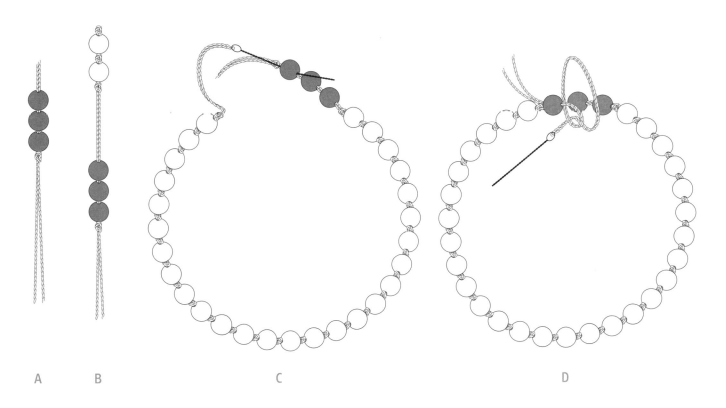

A   B   C   D

E

F

V.
USING CRIMP BEADS TO ATTACH CLASPS

Crimps are little hollow tubes that can be crushed together to grip strands of beading wire. You use them like this.

1. Pass the beading wire through the crimp, then through the loop of the clasp and back through the crimp again. With a pair of crimping pliers or flat-nosed pliers, squeeze the crimp until it firmly grips both strands of the wire (Illus. A and B).

2. Snip off the tail of the wire as close to the crimp as possible (Illus. C).

A slightly more sophisticated finish can be achieved by using crimp covers. These fit over the flattened crimp and are gently squeezed shut to create the look of a normal bead. However, you can only use crimp covers if you have previously used crimping pliers to flatten the crimp.

Another trick is to hide the tail of the beading wire inside an adjacent bead or beads. I always do this if the hole in those beads is big enough to hold two thicknesses of beading wire, and I often add a spacer bead to the end of my design just to permit this method to be used.

1. Pass the beading wire through one or more beads, then through the crimp and through the loop of the clasp.

2. As you bring the beading wire back through the crimp, push it further back through the bead(s).

3. Squeeze the crimp shut, and snip the tail of the wire as close as possible to the last bead it was passed through. This way, the tail end of the beading wire will recoil very slightly and be hidden inside the last bead.

A

B

C

VI.
USING JUMP RINGS AND SPLIT RINGS

HOW TO USE JUMP RINGS

1. With a pair of flat-nosed pliers, grip the jump ring so that it lies flat between the pliers with the join slightly to one side of them.

2. Grip the other side of the join with your fingers. Twist the ring sideways so that it opens.

3. After looping the ring through the piece or pieces you are connecting, close it by once again gripping it with the pliers and twisting the wire back until the two ends meet and the join is closed. Make sure that the two ends of the wire are flush with each other.

Never open jump rings by pulling the ends apart, as they will be much more difficult to close. Always twist them sideways as described above.

HOW TO USE SPLIT RINGS

1. Although you can buy a specialty tool to open these, the simplest way is just to slip your fingernail between the split parts of the ring just behind the opening. This should create just enough space to let you push the piece you wish to connect into the split of the ring.

2. Rotate the ring until the connected item has traveled all the way along the split and out of the opposite side. You may want to use your flat-nosed pliers to help rotate the ring.

VII.
USING HEADPINS
AND EYEPINS

Headpins and eyepins are convenient ways of attaching beads to necklaces, earwires, and other findings. Simply add some beads and make a loop at the top in the following manner:

1. Hold the bottom of the pin to make sure the beads are sitting tightly against it, and cut the top of the pin to the correct length for the loop. For a 3-millimeter loop, there should be a quarter of an inch of pin above the last bead. Small loops are made by gripping the wire toward the tips of the plier jaws. Grip the wire further back to create a larger loop, being sure to allow more wire between the bead and the end of the pin. When you practice this technique, it is useful to make a mark on the jaws of your round-nosed pliers so that you know where to place the wire between the jaws (llus. A).

2. Grip the top of the pin between the jaws of your round-nosed pliers. Make a "P" shape by rolling the pliers away from you. Move the pliers around if necessary until the tip of the pin meets the wire at the top of the bead (llus. B).

3. Put your fingernail behind the neck of the "P," where it touches the bead, and bend the loop back until it is centered above the bead. Your finished loop should look like a balloon with the string hanging straight down (llus. C).

4. To attach the loop to another loop or ring, open it to the side as with the jump ring below.

NOTE

If you are wire-wrapping on a headpin or eyepin, follow the instructions on page 127, substituting the headpin or eyepin for the wire. For larger loops, allow more distance on the wire. Remember, the wire's placement on the jaws of your pliers determines the size of your loop.

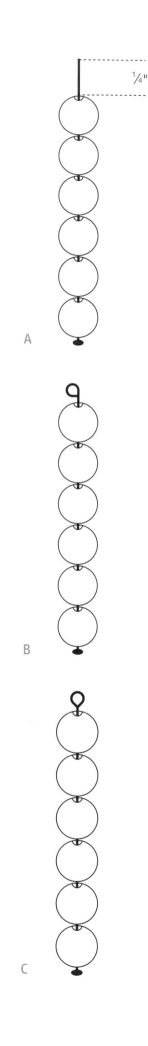

¼"

A

B

C

VIII.
WIRE WRAPPING

This technique can be used with precious metal and other wires or with headpins and eyepins. It forms a stronger loop and adds a space between the loop and the bead. You will need to practice this technique many times to master it. Create a small wire-wrapped loop at each end of a bead in the following manner:

1. Cut a piece of wire to the width of your bead plus about $1\frac{1}{2}$ inches (Illus. A).

2. With round-nosed pliers, grip the wire about $\frac{1}{2}$ inch from the end. Bend the wire around the pliers until a loop is formed and the tail of the wire is perpendicular to the stem (Illus. B).

3. With your fingernail behind the loop, use the round-nosed pliers to roll it back until it is centered above the stem of the wire (Illus. C).

4. Using your finger or fingernail, wrap the tail of the wire around the stem a couple of turns. Use flat-nosed pliers to finish wrapping the tail tightly. Snip off any excess wire (Illus. D, E).

5. Place a bead on the wire. Grip the wire so that the jaws are about $\frac{3}{8}$ inch from the bead, and roll the pliers until a loop is formed and the tail of the wire is perpendicular to the stem (Illus. F, B).

6. With your fingernail behind the loop, roll it back until it is centered above the stem of the wire (Illus. C).

7. Using your finger or fingernail, wrap the tail of the wire around the stem a couple of turns, getting it tight between the bead and the loop. Use flat-nosed pliers to finish wrapping the tail tightly. Snip off any excess wire (Illus. D, E).

NOTE

When making a single loop on a headpin or eyepin, cut the wire about $\frac{5}{8}$" above the bead when making a medium size loop.

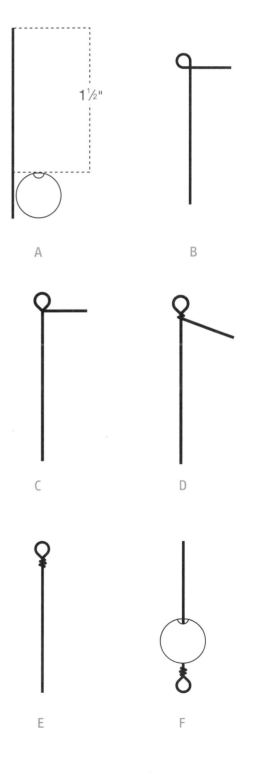

$1\frac{1}{2}$"

A   B

C   D

E   F

STANDARD
MEASUREMENTS

SIZE

The diameter of pearls and other beads is commonly described in millimeters. The chart below shows you the relative sizes from 2 to 16 millimeters.

Since pearls and other beads are often sold in strands measured by the inch, it is useful to know how many beads there are per inch. It is especially useful to know how many pearls there are in a 16-inch strand, a typical length for temporarily strung beads.

LENGTH

One inch = 25.4 millimeters

One foot = 0.3 meters

One millimeter = ¼ inch

One meter = ⅓ foot

WEIGHT

If pearls are large, or if they are sold in great quantities, their weight is sometimes expressed in grains, carats, or grams. The grain standard was originally derived from the weight of one grain of barley or wheat, which gives you an idea of its extreme lightness. Ounces can be very confusing in the world of precious metals or gems. The common ounce used in the United States and Britain is an avoirdupois ounce. Precious metals, on the other hand, are weighed in troy ounces, which are about 10 percent heavier.

THICKNESS

The holes in cultured pearls are commonly .06 millimeter in diameter. Wire thicknesses are measured in American standard gauge or inches or millimeters. Note that the higher the gauge number, the thinner the wire.

Beading wire thicknesses are measured in inches. Note that the last three gauges are roughly equivalent to the beading wire sizes of .018, .015, and .013.

APPROXIMATE NUMBER OF ROUND BEADS IN

		1"	7"	16"	18"
Bead Size	2 mm	12	88	200	225
	3 mm	8	59	134	150
	4 mm	6	44	100	114
	5 mm	5	35	80	90
	6 mm	4	29	67	76
	7 mm	3.5	25	58	65
	8 mm	3	22	50	57
	9 mm	2.5	19	45	40
	10 mm	2.5	17	40	45
	12 mm	2	14	33	38

WEIGHT CONVERSIONS

1 grain = .0648 grams

1 carat = 0.2 grams

1 gram = 5 carats = .03527 ounces = 15.43 grains

1 avoirdupois ounce = 28.35 grams = 437.5 grains

1 troy ounce = 31.1 grams = 480 grains = 1.097 avoirdupois ounces

WIRE THICKNESS

18-gauge = .0403 inches = 1.02 mm

20-gauge = .0320 inches = 0.81 mm

22-gauge = .0253 inches = 0.64 mm

24-gauge = .0201 inches = 0.51 mm

26-gauge = .0159 inches = 0.40 mm

28-gauge = .0126 inches = 0.32 mm

NECKLACE LENGTHS

One of the pleasures of creating your own jewelry is that you can adjust the length of your necklaces so they fit you. A comfortable choker on some necks is a genuine strangler on others, and a centerpiece that is well presented on the faint décolletage of a fashion model might be entirely lost on those who are more generously endowed. If the jewelry is for yourself, disregard the standard lengths and try it on for size as you are making it.

Unless otherwise stated, the necklace ingredients and instructions in this book are for 16-inch necklaces, the so-called "standard" short length. If this length does not suit you, adjust it by adding or subtracting from the ingredients and adjusting the pattern accordingly.

GETTING THE LENGTH RIGHT

Although you can lay out all your pearls in a line and measure them, or place them in the channels of a marked beading board, there is really only one sure way of getting the length right. Just before you think you are halfway through stringing the pearls, hold the uncompleted necklace with the clasp at the back of your neck. Looking in a mirror, you can then judge exactly where the strand will fall. This step is critical in any necklace with a centerpiece or a centered pattern, but it is something I do with every single necklace I am making for myself.

THE "STANDARDS"

Although you will decide the right lengths for your own body, it is useful for jewelry makers to have a general reference guide. There are a variety of opinions about terminology and standard lengths. One woman's "long opera" is another's "rope." The following is as good a guide as any, but remember that the best standard lengths are those you create for yourself. Since a bracelet is, to the maker, just a very short necklace, we start with that length.

Bracelet	7 to 8 inches
Choker	13 to 15 inches
Standard short	16 to 17 inches
Standard long	18 to 20 inches
Matinee	About 24 inches
Opera	30 to 40 inches
Rope	40 inches and over

LENGTH

A 16-inch strand of pearls, knotted with a fish hook clasp will be about 18 inches long when it's finished.

If 18 inches isn't long enough, add a few sterling or gold-filled round beads before the clasp. Or if you are using a hook clasp, add some chain to your bead tip on the opposite side to the hook.

BUYING PEARLS

It is easy to buy pearls nowadays. Bead stores often carry a selection of freshwater pearls, either individually or on temporary strands. There are also mail-order and Internet sellers who have developed a reputation for quality and selection. There are even online auctions. Regardless of where you look, you should understand that the range of quality is very large. It is up to the customer to be discerning.

When you have established your budget, my advice is to go for luster first. It is better to compromise on size or shape or surface blemish than on the one value unique to pearls. Ask these questions:

* How deep is the warm glow from the pearl?
* Are the pearls' body color and overtones pleasing? Do they flatter the color of your skin and eyes?
* Is there any "orient," the iridescent rainbow-like play of light that will attract the attention and admiration your pearls deserve?

If you can answer these questions in the affirmative, or to your satisfaction, chances are you will be happy with your pearls for a very long time, whether they are big or small, round or Baroque.

It is best to examine pearls in good daylight. If the pearls are round or near round, put them on a flat white surface and roll the strand. You will quickly see how close to round they are. You can also detect any thinness in the nacre layers. Parts that are less lustrous than others will show up immediately because the duller patches will seem to "blink" at you. If the pearls are Baroque or another shape, turn the strand round between your hands and look for any unevenness of luster or serious blemishes.

In an inexpensive strand, a few flawed pearls are acceptable; put them at the very back of a necklace or just don't use them. If the pearls seem too perfect and you are worried that they may not be real, try the tooth test (page 133). You can also look at them through a jeweler's loupe (a 10x magnifying glass). Real pearls should show at least some irregularities when magnified.

No matter what the price or category of pearls you are buying, you should first establish that they meet the very basic standards:

* The holes must be drilled straight and centered.

* The nacre must be of a minimum thickness.

* The pearls must be even in appearance.

If the pearls you are considering do not meet these criteria, it is likely that the seller is just trying to clear a job lot of pearl rejects. Do not waste your valuable time on them. No matter how skillful your work, you will end up with something that looks cheap!

If these basic standards are met, you can start evaluating the pearls according to the qualities described on page 24.

CARING FOR PEARLS

Since it is partly composed of organic material, nacre tends to deteriorate over time. Whether the attractive qualities of a pearl last for centuries or for just for years depends both on the thickness of the nacre and on the care with which the pearls are treated. Most pearl sellers coyly suggest that their pearls will last "a lifetime," "for generations," or "for "decades"—as long as they are "properly cared for."

Pearls certainly require more care than other gems. Although you don't have to actively work at keeping them alive, it is good to know what dangers to avoid.

The old adage "a woman should put her pearls on last" is a good one. The wisdom behind this advice is meant to spare the pearls from being coated with perfume, hair spray, or any other cosmetic materials that might hasten their demise. Acid is death to pearls! Cleopatra was said to have dissolved a priceless pearl in wine and drunk it in order to show Mark Anthony that, where extravagance was concerned, she had no equal. (Instead, it ended up being an object lesson in how not to treat a pearl—or an empire.)

Although pearls should be kept away from anything acidic, a little moisture is good for their health. Pearls naturally contain a tiny percentage of water, and they are best preserved in an environment that does not change their composition. Excessive dryness can cause pearls to crack, so store them in a case or pouch lined with soft material somewhere with at least a little humidity. If your skin is acidic, it is a good idea to wipe your pearls with a damp cloth after wearing. A little olive oil can also be good for pearls if you feel like pampering them.

In general, however, you should simply keep your pearls away from acidic or corrosive substances. Do not store them in an excessively dry place or in a box with a bunch of other jewelry that might damage their surface. Of course, try not to drop them on hard surfaces or scratch them. And remember, cats and children have no business playing with your pearls!

FAUX PEARLS

*She passed him the necklace, the weight of which she
had gathered for a moment into her hand. He measured
it in the same way with his own, but remained quite
detached. "Worth at most thirty shillings."
"Not more?"
"Surely not if it's paste?"
"But IS it paste?"
He gave a small sniff of impatience. "Pearls nearly as
big as filberts?"
"But they're heavy," Charlotte declared.
"No heavier than anything else."
"Do you imagine for a moment they're real?"
She studied them a little, feeling them, turning them
round. "Mightn't they possibly be?"
—"Paste," Henry James, 1909*

I read Henry James's short story "Paste" when I was a girl and
immediately sympathized with the character Charlotte's viewpoint.
Why shouldn't the pearls be real? Not only did I dislike the masculine
cynicism of this passage, but I hated the word "paste." It sounded like
glue, not jewelry. The word is derived from the softness of the glass
used to imitate gems and has, thankfully, long since been replaced
by "faux."

"Faux" (pronounced "foh") is just a fancy French word for "false" or
"fake," but since it sounds so elegant, it is the fashionable word for
imitation gems.

People have been trying to make imitation pearls for as long as the
real ones have been treasured. In a way, all beads seek to imitate
pearls which, after all, must have been the original delight of jewelers
and wearers alike—a pretty, round object on a string.

In the seventeenth century, a Frenchman called Jaquin discovered a
neat trick. By coating glass beads with a mixture of ground-up fish
scales and varnish, he produced an effect similar to the iridescence
and luster of a pearl. So good was this imitation that the fish-scale
mixture, known as "pearl essence," has been used ever since to make
high-quality imitation pearls.

The essence of "pearl essence" is a substance called guanine, which gives fish scales their color. The collection of these scales from herring and other fish has provided an important supplementary income to many fisheries for more than two centuries. Today synthetic pearl essence is produced through a chemical process. Curiously, pearl essence, also known as "essence d'orient," is also used to produce sparkle in some lipsticks and eye shadows.

CHANEL

Perhaps we owe the modern respectability of faux pearls to that great couturier, Coco Chanel. A lover of pearls, she pronounced the dictum that a woman needs "ropes and ropes" of pearls, which helped expand their place in the world of contemporary fashion. Her simple black sweater with many strands of pearls created a look that was both understated simplicity and voluptuous extravagance. Of course, very few 1920s women could afford a string of pearls, let alone a rope. But Chanel's fashions made no impossible demands. If one had money, the pearls were real. If one didn't, then they were paste—or, even better, "faux!"

TESTING FOR "FAUX"

Imitation pearls can often be good enough to fool the eye, but they never imitate the feel of a real pearl. The classic way to test a pearl is to rub it against your tooth. A glass pearl will feel smooth and slide easily over the enamel of your teeth. A real pearl will feel gritty and quite unpleasant. Try this test very gently on your real pearls, as the very act of rubbing one of these gems against your tooth might damage the nacre.

PEARL DRILLING

Even parts of the world which have never seen a living pearl mollusk play special niche roles in this global industry. In a village outside of Hyderabad, a landlocked city in India, some 500 families are solely occupied by the job of drilling pearls. A delicate job, requiring a considerable degree of skill, drilling pearls provides an income for many thousands of people in many different countries. It also provides an additional benefit—pearl powder.

Although the holes of pearls are only a few tenths of a millimeter wide, the powdered pearl from the drilling process is carefully collected and used in a variety of medicines and cosmetics. In much of the orient, creams containing powdered pearl are considered to be particularly efficacious in maintaining a fair complexion, as if the lustrous beauty of the pearl can be transferred directly to the skin.

YOUR GRANDMOTHER'S PEARLS

If you are fortunate, you may have a strand or two of pearls in the family that have been passed down from your grandmother or some other benevolent relative. Perhaps the strands have been hidden away, half scorned because of their drooping, gap-ridden appearance. Perhaps the necklace looks tired or old fashioned. But the pearls are fresh and always in fashion-and it is the pearls which are the real prize, not the necklace.

So begin deconstructing. Look at the loose pearls as a newly discovered treasure trove. Who knows? If they are old enough they may even be that rare gem, an entirely natural pearl. And even if they are cultured, as long as the nacre is thick enough, they could have generations to go before they lose their luster. Buy a new clasp, something a bit expensive that really talks to you—after all, you didn't have to pay for the pearls!

Lay out the pearls. You might be able to shorten the strand a bit and steal a couple for earrings. Use your newly discovered talent for knotting, spend a pleasant hour putting it all together, and suddenly you will have a new star in your jewelry collection—a piece wholly your own.

RESOURCES

The pearls, beads, and findings for these projects and can be found online at www.beadworks.com.

Bead stores have been opening (and closing) at such a rapid pace that it is best to use the Internet or a phone directory to find them. Always call the store first to ask what kind of pearl selection they have in stock. It is frustrating to drive dozens of miles with coin pearls in mind, only to find out that there is no more than a meager selection of tiny rice pearls.

There are several Internet directories of bead stores, including www.guidetobeadwork.com and www.beadwork.about.com.

A number of publications serve the bead customer and have large resource listings:
Bead & Button magazine: www.beadandbutton.com
Lapidary Journal: www.lapidaryjournal.com
Beadwork magazine: www.interweave.com/bead/beadwork_magazine

The following websites are well worth visiting if only to see their beautiful examples of the finest pearls and faux pearls:

www.paspaleypearls.com (for South Sea pearls)
www.mikimoto.com (for Akoya pearls)
www.perlesdetahiti.net (for Tahitian black pearls)
www.americanpearlcompany.com (for American freshwater peals)
www.create-your-style.com (for faux pearls)

In 2002, the American Museum of Natural History created an exhibition about pearls that proved so popular that it is now touring museums worldwide.
An abridged view of the exhibition can be seen online at www.amnh.org/exhibitions/pearls.

If you are inspired by the designs in this book but too busy to make them yourself, visit www.NancyAlden.com for a range of made-up pearl jewelry.

ACKNOWLEDGMENTS

All the jewelry in this book was created by Nancy Alden except for contributions from these fine designers:

Jennifer Wechsler—Pearls with Green Garnets

Susan Moffat—Floating Pearls Necklace

Kate Parisi—Stick Pearls and "Cornflakes"

Sarah Young—Seed Pearl Earrings & Coin Pearl Earrings

Brandi Lawrence—Chandelier Earrings

Thanks also to the following people for their work on the book:

Joseph De Leo, photography

Gigi Scandinaro, styling

Devon Cutrin, cover modeling and photo assistance

Emily Rae and Miki Onoroto, jewelry design assistance

Liz Doughty. Ivannia Gomez, jewelry components coordination

Parvin Khan, pearl sourcing

Stephen Sammons, research

Everyone at Potter Craft, including Lauren Monchik, Elizabeth Wright, Amy Sly, Christina Schoen, and Isa Loundon

I would like to express my long-term appreciation for my partner and friend, Tony Alers-Hankey, who initiated a global business that would supply jewelry designers like me with endless inspiration and possibilities. Although he would be the first to admit he stumbled upon the concept of an open-display bead store, it was his commitment, faith, and foresight that led to its success. He is truly "the elder statesman" of the business of beads.

I would like to thank Carson Eddy, whose fine operation of Boston's Beadworks led Shawna Mullen to seek us out and convince me to write this book. Without Shawna's editorial hand-holding and prodding, the project could not have been conceived.

Above all, I would like to thank all of my colleagues and the many thousands of customers whose great enthusiasm for creating jewelry has been the inspiration of my career.

This book is dedicated to Janet Wall whose spirit of adventure caused it all to happen.

PROJECT INDEX

This illustrated guide is organized by project type, so you can quickly locate a project that suits your mood and materials.

BRACELETS

Pearl and Marcasite Rondel Bracelet, page 68

Pearl "Berries" Bracelet, page 104

Pearl Silver Bracelet, page 105

Ruby and Pearl Bracelet, page 106

EARRINGS

Chain Earrings with Pearl Drops, page 49

Mother-of-Pearl Earrings, page 88

Faux Pearl and Chain Earrings, page 89

Tahitian Pearl Earrings, page 89

Potato Pearl and Chain Earrings, page 90

Round Pearl and Chain Earrings, page 91

Coin Pearl and Chain Earrings, page 91

Seed Pearl Earrings, page 94

Coin Pearl Earrings, page 95

Blue-and-Green Pearl Earrings, page 95

Chandelier Earrings, page 96

Horizontal Stick Pearl Earrings, page 97

Vertical Stick Pearl Earrings, page 97

NECKLACES

Sweet Sixteen Necklace, page 32

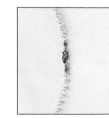

The Classic, page 32

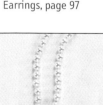

Big-Girl Pearls, page 33

Fabulous Faux, page 33

The Classic Three-Strand
Necklace, page 36

Multistrand Keshi Pearl
Necklace, page 37

Rich Girl's Pearls,
page 40

Floating Pearls
Necklace, page 41

Single-Strand Necklace,
page 44

Double-Strand Necklace,
page 45

Faux Pearls with Chain,
page 48

Lariat with Chain and
Pearl Drops, page 49

Pearls with Green
Garnets, page 58

Pearl Strand with Gem
Cluster, page 62

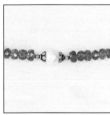
Gemstones with Pearl
Centerpiece, page 63

Prima Ballerina
Necklace, page 64

Pearl and Tourmaline
Necklace, page 65

Crystal and Pearl
Necklace, page 69

Pearls with Charlottes,
page 72

Pearls and Daisies,
page 73

Stick Pearls and
"Cornflakes," page 76

Stick Pearls with Bali
Beads, page 77

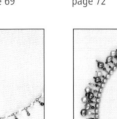
Faceted Pearls on Wire,
page 80

A Lot of Work —
But Worth It!, page 81

Pearls on Leather Cord,
page 84

Pearls on Snake Chain,
page 85

Keshi Pearl Lariat,
page 100

Coin Pearl Lariat,
page 101

Pearl and Turquoise
Eyeglass Leash,
page 107

INDEX

ABOUT THE AUTHOR

Nancy Alden Wall (who writes and designs under the name Nancy Alden) is a jewelry designer and cofounder of the Beadworks Group, one of world's largest retailers of beads. As Beadworks' principal buyer and designer, she travels the world in search of the most beautiful components for jewelry design. She is equally at home with gemstone merchants in Jaipur, silver makers in Bali, and glass artists in Bohemia as she is with pearl producers in China. Her knowledge of beads and findings is unrivalled, spanning all categories of material and all stages of production from the creation of a single bead to its final role in a finished piece of jewelry.

Starting as a silver and goldsmith, Nancy turned to designing with beads because of the vastly greater possibilities for creative expression. Having seen the world of jewelry design open for herself, she then went on to introduce other people to the creative pleasures and the economies of making their own jewelry. By creating Beadworks' classes and sharing her skills with other instructors, she has generated a network of teachers who have added to the ever-growing number of women and men able to design and create jewelry. Now, for the first time, she shares her design and production techniques in a fully comprehensive and easy to follow guide, enabling an even wider audience to make their own attractive necklaces, earrings and bracelets. When she is not in search of new beads, Nancy divides her time between her home in Connecticut and studio retreats in Europe and the Grenadines.

ABOUT BEADWORKS

In 1978, a small store in London began selling a very ancient product in a very novel way. Although beads are among the very earliest of traded articles, the concept of offering a large, sophisticated, and open display to the general public was new.

The shop never advertised—indeed, it didn't even have a name for many years—but the demand for its product was immediate and overwhelming. Simply by word of mouth, the original store became world famous.

With American jewelry designer, Nancy Alden Wall, the concept expanded to North America, where it has grown to half a dozen stores and a mail order business. Beadworks has inspired people from around the world to open their own bead stores, enabling hundreds of thousands of people to make their own jewelry. You can visit Beadworks online at www.beadworks.com.